AIRLINE

A STRATEGIC MANAGEMENT SIMULATION

4TH EDITION

Jerald R. Smith
and
Peggy A. Golden
Graduate School of Business
Florida Atlantic University

Vivek Patel
Technical Consultant

Special Consultants
Bryce Appleton
Former CEO, Midway Airline

Michael Forte
Airline Captain

Prentice
Hall

Upper Saddle River, New Jersey 07458

Acquisitions Editor: Melissa Steffens
Editor-in-Chief: Jeff Shelstad
Assistant Editor: Jessica Sabloff
Editorial Assistant: Kevin Glynn
Media Project Manager: Michele Faranda
Marketing Manager: Shannon Moore
Managing Editor (Production): Judy Leale
Production Editor: Marcela Maslanczuk
Production Assistant: Dianne Falcone
Permissions Coordinator: Suzanne Grappi
Associate Director, Manufacturing: Vincent Scelta
Production Manager: Arnold Vila
Manufacturing Buyer: Diane Peirano
Design Manager: Patricia Smythe
Cover Design: Bruce Kenselaar
Cover Illustration/Photo: TonyStone Images/Mark Wagner
Associate Director, Multimedia Production: Karen Goldsmith
Manager, Print Production: Christy Mahon
Printer/Binder: Victor Graphics

Prentice Hall

10 9 8 7 6 5 4 3 2
ISBN 0-13-065488-4

CONTENTS

INDEX

iv

ACKNOWLEDGMENTS

Simulation games such as *Airline: A Strategic Management Simulation* become realities only because of the cooperation of many people and organizations. We wish to acknowledge some of the individuals and groups that gave their time and expertise in the development of this simulation. Special thanks go to many kind people. Bryce Appleton, former CEO and owner of Midstate Airlines, for his willingness to teach us the commuter/regional airline business. Although we have taken some author license with the cost relationships in the interest of building a balanced educational experience, our fundamental understanding of the business was a result of the participation of Bryce and his staff at the airline.

A special thanks to the management team at Florida Atlantic University's College of Business and Graduate School of Business for encouraging simulation technology: Dean Bruce Mallen, Darab Unwalla, and Dennis Coates.

We also appreciate the many professors in the academic field who believe in the unique benefits of learning through simulations, including Joseph Peyrefitte, Mark Meckler, Peter Goumas, Joe Wolfe, Bernie Keys, Marshall Schminke, Howard Feldman, Wayne Koprowski, Herman Wassons, Ron Ryan, Jenniver Ettling, Chunyan Yu, Ron Spense, Steve Harrington, Miguel Hidalo, Douglas Marshal, Jaou Merkt, Tina DeBrass, Margaret O'Rouke-Kelly, Pierre Louis Agnes, Jerry Terrell, David Ackerman, John Myhre, Virginia Smiley, Ronald Levy, William March, Cliff Ingari, and J. Bakki.

If you are an *Airline* user and would care to join our cadre of special professors when the manual is printed again, please e-mail us.

There is a unique organization in which we encourage your membership. It is the main source of simulation information for academicians. It holds an annual meeting and publishes newsletters. It is the International Association of Business Simulations and Experiential Learning (ABSEL). You may contact it at www.towson.edu/~absel.

Finally, we are blessed with a wonderful extended family who sometimes wonders why we stay up so late when developing simulations. We answer, "We have the simulation disease!" Many thanks to David, Flossie, Jennifer, Matthew, Susan, Willie, Barbara, Michael, and Charles.

Jerald Smith   *Peggy Golden*

Contacting the Authors

Please check the Instructor's Manual for our e-mail addresses and phone numbers. We are always happy to correspond with instructors but due to our workloads, cannot answer student inquiries.

System Requirements

Pentium or equivalent. Windows 95, 98, NT. 32 MB Ram. 30 MB available hard disk space. Floppy drive if used with student disk entry. VGA Color Display.

QUICK GUIDE TO COSTS AND OTHER COMMON VALUES

Revenues

Commissions paid to travel agents	10% of the value of the ticket
on 80% of gross revenues which calculates to	8% of gross revenues

Operating Expenses

Insurance: # seats in plane w/20 seats or less	$180 per seat × number of seats
# seats in plane w/> 20 seats	$300
Marketing expenses, includes Advertising and Promotion budgets + $12,000 for each salesperson	
Market research studies: Entire package costs	$31,000 (Full list on page 14)
Hiring and cost of acquiring a new employee	$3,000

Financial

Short-term loan, beginning rate	10% per annum or 2.5% per quarter
Long-term loan, fixed rate throughout simulation	9% per annum or 2.25% per quarter
Interest paid on CDs	5% per annum or 1.25% per quarter
Lease payment found on page 12	
Cost to purchase an aircraft on page 12	
Administrative expense	$100,000 for up to 76 seats
	$150,000 for up to 102 seats
	other levels on page 26
Depreciation	2% per quarter per aircraft owned
	+ $5000 on facilities and equipment
Income tax	40% of net profits
Cost to sell an aircraft	2% of book value
Cost to break a lease	$50,000 per aircraft
Accounts receivable	40% of gross revenues
Accounts payable	30% of gross revenues

Flight Operations

Cost to enter a new market	$10,000
Flight operations cost per mile	12¢
Fuel is posted on quarterly report	$1.00 per gallon at beginning
Maintenance: Level 1	no additional charges
Level 2	$2,500 per aircraft per quarter
Level 3	$3,500 per aircraft per quarter

Cabin service costs are $1, $2, and $5.

Sale on fares: Usually an entry of 1, which is 1/3 off ticket prices for one month.

Flight attendants: Need one if >30 seats. The cost is built into "flight operations" cost.

Demand forecast: Is just a forecast, not a guaranteed rate of demand increase or decrease.

SECTION 1
THE DECISION MAKING PROCESS

> This section contains all information needed to make decisions in the simulation. Before reading this section, refer to a Decision form [which is the last item in the manual] to get an overview of all the decisions your team will be making.

HISTORY OF THE AIRLINE

The airline you are taking over is no stranger to thousands of people living in small communities scattered throughout the United States. Like other commuter airlines, the company has been providing air service to cities and towns that were unattractive to large carriers because of the population size or the limited facilities at the local airport.

This airline was established as a "mom-and-pop" business to fill the void left by a larger regional airline that abandoned the area. The airline grew from a fledgling carrier that transported 2,700 passengers in its first year to a regional airline that is now carrying over 16,000 passengers annually. The case contained at the back of this manual, Mid-Continent Airlines, was included to give you a better idea of the point at which you are taking over the management of this airline. The present fleet consists of three 19 passenger Beech 1900 aircraft. These are real workhorses but without toilet facilities, should not be used in longer flights nor luxury service.

In 1978, the Federal government deregulated the entire airline industry leaving all companies able to compete for customers by creating competitive fare structures and competitive routes. One response by major carriers was to diminish service to the less profitable markets and create hubs in large cities. Commuter airlines jumped in to fill the service vacuums left in many medium-sized cities.

Today, as a member of the Airline Reporting Corporation (ARC) your airline has interline ticketing and baggage arrangements with all major carriers. The agreement allows the airline to issue tickets to any destination and to check baggage through to the final destination.

The operating history of the airline you are taking over has been one of slow growth over a 16 year period. Selected operating and financial information for the past two years is shown at a later point in this manual. However, the past lackluster performance of the airline is history. You are purposely not being furnished with a great deal of past financial data because the industry is now deregulated and new opportunities are available that the former management did not have.

The manual is arranged in the same order as the decision form for ease in making decisions..

PREPARING THE DECISION FORM

The next section describes how to fill out the decision form. Since the simulation cannot be changed once it is "run," it is critical that your team enter decisions correctly. A decision form is shown on the last page of the manual.

DECISION 1: FARES

FARE: per seat mile flown (Do not use a decimal) _____ **cents**

> This is an average of all types of fares the airline may have. You can determine the effect on a specific market of raising or lowering the fare by multiplying this figure by the number of miles in the market. For example, a ticket in a market of 400 miles = 400 × .35 = $140.00. Increasing the fare to 38 cents would be calculated as: 400 x .38 = $152.00. However, demand will be somewhat lower with the higher fare.

TABLE 1
FARE STRUCTURE

Discount Airline	.28 to .31
Normal range	.35 to .40
Luxury Airline	.48 to .51

✔ Last quarter the firm charged 35 cents per mile for its fare.

Do not attempt to price between these ranges as the decision entry program will not accept values not listed above. A firm may use the sale on fares feature of the simulation to provide an exceptional fare to selected markets. This will be discussed in the MARKETS section later in the manual.

Explanation

Airline fares are one of the more complex pricing systems in the free enterprise world. All airlines post a standard fare and then may offer special discounts on that fare. In addition, airlines develop a sale on fares from time to time when opening a new market or to boost sluggish demand. A sale on fares stimulates demand but reduces revenues. The competitive market is very reactive to fare changes; thus fare reductions tend to be copied by competitors and the benefits to a single airline are short-lived.

The fare for your airline will be an average of all of your fares on a _seat mile flown_ basis. This amount is a reflection of your pricing strategy, ranging from a discount airline to a premium service policy. Your airline has been charging fares of 35 cents per seat-mile-flown. While the current fare of 35 cents per passenger mile has been generating enough revenue for the current small fleet, the higher costs of purchasing or leasing additional planes may require a higher fare structure. However you must always take into consideration what fares your competition is charging.

For an airline to become a discount airline in your simulated industry, it would need to price between 28 and 31 cents. As a low-cost producer, it should watch expenses carefully. There is room for at least one discount airline in your industry. At the other end of the spectrum we have the luxury airline. A few airlines have attempted luxury service in the real world and some have been successful. To be successful, the highest level of cabin service and maintenance must be maintained. There is room in the simulated industry for at least one _high-end_ competitor. Demand is not as high but the additional revenues should provide satisfactory profits; you MUST use cabin class aircraft (C to G) and cabin service choice 3 to build a luxury image. In order to price correctly, a team wishing to discount or become a luxury carrier must set their fares within the ranges shown in Table 1. Both discounters and luxury airlines must not fly too many flights in any one market, as there is limited demand for the specialized type of services.

DECISION 2: CABIN SERVICE   (Enter a 0, 1, 2, or 3) _____

> This item is your choice of the type of cabin service and food/drinks that are served on your flight. It is not feasible to offer cabin service on aircraft that are not listed as Cabin Class, as the headroom is not adequate. However, preboarding and postflight food and beverages could be provided in the case of noncabin class flights.

The following table indicates the choices available for cabin service and the current costs.

TABLE 2
CABIN SERVICE COST

Decision Key		Cost per Passenger Flown
0	No cabin service	0
1	Free soft drinks, and pretzels or peanuts	$1.00
2	Free soft drinks, snacks, and small snack meal for Flights commencing between 6 and 8 A.M., 12 to 1P.M., and 6-7 P.M. (Includes carry-your-own on noncabin class aircraft - Type A)	$2.00
	This cost is pro-rated for flights not providing snacks, so the cost shown is charged to all passengers for easier simulation accounting.	
3	Free drinks & hors d'oeuvres on or before all flights. Meal service as required.	$5.00

Explanation

Cabin service includes your choice of food and beverage service on flights. It is not feasible to offer cabin service on aircraft types A or B, as the headroom is not adequate and these two aircraft types do not require a cabin attendant. However, preboarding and postflight food and beverages would be provided and/or a box lunch could be furnished to each passenger as they board, in the case of noncabin class flights. In terms of relative demand, there would be a slight sales advantage to a firm that had cabin service on a route versus a competitor that did not. However, if all firms serving a route had the same level of cabin service, none would have a sales advantage. Cabin service is representative of an overall corporate philosophy and applies to your entire fleet. In other words, whatever level of cabin service you choose becomes a blanket policy for all your routes.

Federal Aviation Administration regulations require an attendant on all flights utilizing aircraft with 30 seats or more. The additional labor cost of the attendant(s) is included in the operating cost of the larger aircraft and you do not need to calculate or enter this on the decision form. If your team desires, you may assume the sale of alcoholic beverages on cabin service levels 1, 2, or 3. Since the simulation assumes round trip tickets, the cost of cabin service is two times the number of seats sold.

> ### *DIFFERENCES IN STUDENT MANUAL EDITIONS*
> This edition was printed after the original manual was printed. Several clarifications and numerical changes were made which will not show up on the first printing, which is usually a used book. Do not be surprised if a team mate has a manual that is different. He/she should return the manual to the bookstore and obtain a new manual.

DECISION 3 - PROMOTION BUDGET   (Enter in $ with no commas) $_____

DECISION 4 - ADVERTISING BUDGET   (Enter in $ with no commas) $_____

> These two budget items are crucial to your firm's strategy. Last quarter the airline budgeted $2,500 for promotion and $2,500 for advertising.

Explanation

All airlines spend a significant amount of money to attract passengers. A unique aspect of this industry, however, is that much promotional activity is targeted at online travel services and other specialists who dispose of extra seats. These sources combined with travel agents, are responsible 75% of the tickets sold. Promotions include packaged vacations, incentive plans for travel agents selling large numbers of tickets, frequent flyer programs, familiarization (FAM) trips for travel agents, etc. Discounted tickets and special fares are not included in this budget but are in the "sale on fares" decision which is available on a market-by-market basis. Some airlines also sell their tickets directly from a Web site which reduces the transaction cost somewhat without affecting the fare charged. If you want to sell tickets from a third party Web site, you must include at least $7,502 in the promotion budget EACH quarter. However, this may be changed by your response to Incident C.

Airlines also advertise through the various media: billboards, magazines, television, radio, and newspapers. The allocation of the advertising and promotion budgets is a reflection of the target market for each airline. Those firms trying to attract the business traveler will use different media than those that are after the casual traveler. Some companies participate in customized "in-flight" magazines placed on board the aircraft to enhance and promote image.

Last quarter, your company spent $2,500 on promotional and $2,500 on advertising activities; this is a very minimal amount. As your fleet increases you will need to budget substantially more. You have not been producing an on-board magazine for your passengers; the cost for this would be $500 per aircraft per quarter in addition to your normal advertising budget. To indicate you want to produce an on-board magazine, enter a 1 as the right-hand digit in your advertising budget EACH quarter plus your normal advertising budget (example: $2,500 advertising + [10 A/C * $500 each] = 7501).

DECISION 5: NUMBER OF NEW SALESPERSONS HIRED THIS QUARTER _____

> Your firm does not have any sales force now due to its small size. However, as you grow you may want to add salespersons. The maximum you can hire or fire in a quarter is 4.

Explanation

The cost of each salesperson is $12,000 per quarter, which includes the employee's salary, travel allowance, and fringe benefits. Airlines employ a sales force to act as a go-between in promoting business with corporations and travel agents. One advantage of building a sales force, in addition to additional sales, is the possibility of a greater volume of direct sales to corporations and tour promoters, thus lowering the amount paid for commissions to travel agents.

✔ Once hired, you do not enter salespersons on the payroll in this space or the program will continue to hire more! (The total number of salespersons is tracked by the program.)

✔ Use a minus sign to discharge salespersons. You may not hire or fire more than four salespersons per quarter.

DECISION 6: EMPLOYEE COMPENSATION POLICY _____

> Your airline is now paying the average wages for a regional airline. This budget item is for wages and fringes above the normal wage. The airline has never made additional payments to its employees.

TABLE 3
EMPLOYEE COMPENSATION POLICY

0 = Pay prevailing wages for regional airlines
1 = Managers and pilots receive ___% above minimum prevailing wages
2 = Pay ____% above minimum prevailing wages to pilots.
3 = Pay ____% above minimum to all employees including pilots and professionals
4 = Pay ____% above minimum to professionals + stock-bonus
5 = Pay ____% above minimum to all employees + stock-bonus
6 = Pay ____% above minimum to professionals + 20% of profits
7 = Pay ____% above minimum + 20% profits to all employees

Explanation

You may increase wages and/or other benefits such as a stock-bonus plan and a profit-sharing plan. At this time the firm does not pay any of these additional sums. It is operating on a shoestring budget and paying minimal wages to most personnel. Although not making any additional expenditures adds to employee turnover (currently 8% per quarter) and additional hiring as well as on-the-job training (OJT) costs, former management felt this was the best in the past.

An Added Note on Employee Compensation

Your employee compensation has an effect on retention as well as your ability to attract the optimal work force for your airline. Although many of the employees available to you are young and willing to work for lower wages, they see the opportunities at larger airlines and treat you as a training environment. More stable employees cost more but will not change jobs as readily. Some research indicates that a sense of ownership created by profit-sharing and stock-bonus plans assists in employee retention. This airline has historically paid prevailing (minimal) industry wages to its pilots, station managers, and maintenance people. Salaried professionals (company officers) are paid slightly over the minimum market wage for these categories.

DECISION 7: WAGE INCREASE to Accompany Decision 6
Enter % wage increase (if applicable) _____%

> This item is used in conjunction with Decision 6. If managers and pilots are to be given an additional sum, you may base the cost on $100,000 in quarterly wages per aircraft operated. If pilots only are to be given a wage increase, base the additional compensation on $40,000 in quarterly wages per aircraft.

Explanation

An example for a 5% wage increase to managers and pilots follows:

3 aircraft × $100,000 = $300,000 × .05 = $15,000 added cost per quarter

If ALL employees are to be given an additional sum, base the total wages on $140,000 per aircraft operated. Example of 4% to all employees: Three aircraft x $140,000 = $420,000 x .04 = $16,800 added cost per quarter.

You may add a stock-bonus plan to a wage increase or grant the stock-bonus plan without a wage increase (by placing a zero in the wage increase enter line). The cost of the stock-bonus plan is based on the number of employees required to operate each aircraft in the fleet, but for simplicity the cost is set at $5,000 per aircraft operated. Employee compensation is charged for the cost of this stock. In addition, the "stock sold" account on the cash flow statement shows the sale of the stock to the employee stock fund. The shares of stock outstanding will also increase due to the sale of this stock.

The final option (either with or without an accompanying wage increase) is a profit-sharing plan. It is based on 20% of the previous quarter's profits and the actual cost is charged; if there are no profits, none can be distributed and there is no cost.

✔ The amount of additional compensation (e.g., 2%, 3%) must be entered each quarter. The program DOES NOT carry over previous decisions. Once a given level of additional employee compensation is started, you should make every attempt to maintain it, since employee morale would be hurt by giving something one quarter and lowering it the next.

✔ A Tip: If you do pay additional wages, start modestly and increase pay as your profits increase (for example .5% or 1%).

DECISION 8 - QUALITY PROGRAMS AND ADDITIONAL TRAINING (even $) $_____

> This budget is to provide additional training to employees and to create a quality management program. Last quarter the airline budgeted $1,000 for extra training. The right hand digit of this entry is reserved to indicate a merger so enter in even dollars such as 1,000, 5000, 8,000, etc. See page 34.

Explanation

The regulatory environment of the airline industry requires some on-the-job training for flight crews and other employees. In addition, some firms offer additional training and development to increase employee competence, increase customer satisfaction, and create commitment to high-quality service. Average training and development costs are $40 per employee per half-day workshop. Therefore, if you want to provide a four hour seminar for 40 employees, the cost would be $1,600. A direct benefit of employee (and thus organizational) development activities is that they seem to be related to retention of personnel, which can also affect the reliability of your airline.

✔ Your airline paid $1,000 last quarter for additional employee training. (Remember, this amount is in addition to the legally required training of flight crews and maintenance personnel.)

Quality Programs

In addition to training, your firm may want to initiate quality programs. You may initiate such programs on a department-by-department basis or all at one time (which would be considered a Total Quality Management system). Programs cost $5,000 per quarter per department. There are four major departments to consider: customer service, aircraft servicing, maintenance, and administrative. Thus, to start a program for the entire company would cost a minimum of $20,000 per quarter. If you want to emphasize quality even more, you may budget more than this amount. Once you start a quality program, you should continue it indefinitely.

Quality Index

The public's perception of your firm, in terms of quality, will be published each quarter as a *Quality Index*. Your actual quality may be higher than this index, but it represents how the public perceives your airline. **A reminder**: You must add your quality budget to your additional training budget and enter the total amount each quarter.

✓ DECISION 9: AIRCRAFT MAINTENANCE LEVEL (Enter 1, 2, or 3) ____

> The minimum required maintenance (Level 1) permits you to fly with some assurances of dependability. However, the higher levels (2 or 3) can increase reliability somewhat as well as create a higher company image. Currently the firm is operating at Level 1.

The three levels of maintenance are:

LEVEL 1: Legal minimum maintenance; normal interior cleaning of aircraft. Exterior cleaning every 9 months. Reasonable parts inventory.

LEVEL 2: Legal minimum maintenance, some additional interior cleaning of the aircraft's interior; exterior cleaning of the aircraft every 6 months; and an additional 20% of spare parts in inventory, which should result in less downtime for repairing aircraft. The current added cost of this level is $2,500 per aircraft per quarter.

LEVEL 3: Legal minimum maintenance, more frequent interior cleaning of the aircraft; exterior cleaning every 3 months; an additional 40% of spare parts in inventory, and a full preventive maintenance program. The current additional cost of this level is $3,500 per aircraft per quarter.

Explanation

Federal regulatory agencies specify a minimal level of maintenance for aircraft. In addition, each manufacturer provides a required maintenance schedule based on the maintenance record of each model of aircraft. Recent articles in aviation periodicals suggest that consumers are affected by the overall appearance of the craft, including external and cabin cleanliness.

The fewer types of aircraft you have, the lower your maintenance costs will be. As different types of aircraft are added, a greater number of parts must be stocked, mechanics must be trained to work on a new type, and specialized tools and equipment must be procured. It should be noted that Level 1 is a very safe level of maintenance. Many airlines adhere to this level and have very good safety and reliability records. However, other firms believe that higher levels of maintenance enhance their overall reliability record and customer image.

DECISION 10: FUEL CONTRACT for Next Quarter (Enter 0, 1, or 2) _____

> Fuel costs are one of the largest line items in the expense statement. There are three options for purchasing fuel; they are listed below.

0 = All fuel purchased on the spot market this quarter
1 = 50% purchased on open market and 50% on contract
2 = All fuel purchased on contract this quarter

✔ You may switch from one type of fuel purchase to another from one quarter to the next. There is no penalty for doing so.

Explanation

This item is one of the most unpredictable expenses incurred in operations. Fuel can be purchased either on the open market (as needed at various airports) or on a three-month contract that holds a fixed rate. The contract price can either be somewhat higher or lower than the "spot" price at the time the contract is negotiated, depending on the forecasted price of fuel for the next quarter. Your fuel has been purchased on the open market the past quarter. [Fuel prices in the simulation may not equate to prices in the "real world" due to the variability of prices there. They have been set in relation to other variables.]

DECISION 11: CARGO BUDGET   (Enter $ 0 - $50,000 no comma) $_____

> Currently, your company is not in the cargo business. You may choose to enter the cargo business at any time, or not at all. To begin hauling cargo on your passenger planes, you will need to enter a budget for marketing your new service and decide if you want to hire one or more salespersons to sell your cargo services.

Explanation

To simplify matters, the simulation assumes that cargo will be loaded into the cargo bays of the aircraft up to the maximum takeoff weight of the aircraft. However, passengers will not be bumped to make room for cargo. In case there are more passengers and cargo than the aircraft can handle, the excess cargo will be held until the next flight out or placed on another carrier. Thus, as you become more successful in filling your aircraft with passengers, you will have less room for cargo. There is no provision in the simulation for having an all-cargo aircraft.

If you want to initiate your cargo service, you must budget at least $10,000 per quarter for added overhead. To add a salesperson whose sole duty is to sell cargo services, you must <u>add</u> $12,000 to the cargo marketing budget for each salesperson (in addition to any advertising). NOTE: This salesperson is not included in passenger salespersons hired, but included only in your "Cargo Marketing Budget." The reason for this is that salespersons involved in selling passenger service are calling a different type of customer (e.g., mainly travel agents) and so they cannot be used in cargo sales, as this is a very specialized business. You may hire as many salespersons as you think you need and the budget must be entered every quarter. Your net profit after direct cargo expenses will be shown on the income statement. As in any new service, it will take some time to build up your cargo service and produce a profit.

✔ For example, if you want one cargo salesperson and $2,000 in cargo advertising, you would enter $24,000 each quarter (Overhead $10,000 + Salesperson $12,000 + Advertising $2,000).

✔ If you fail to enter your cargo budget, when you do begin again you will need to "build up" your image and presence which will take at least 3 quarters.

DECISION 12: CORPORATE SOCIAL PERFORMANCE BUDGET $_____

> Social responsibility is an important aspect of any business. A firm has a responsibility to many *publics* in addition to its stockholders: employees, suppliers, creditors, competitors, government, the local community, and the ecological environment. The firm has never budgeted funds for this item.

Explanation

The budget for this area will provide funds for the social responsibility of your firm. In addition to the amount budgeted, you may choose to target a specific area where the budget is to be used. Use the key numbers listed below and enter the key as the right-hand digit of your budget ($4,001 or $10,006, etc.). You may budget any amount in even thousands, with a $1,000 minimum. The examples for each category are meant to be broad categories and not specific items. Last quarter the firm did not budget any funds for these programs.

Social Responsibility Areas of Concentration

1 = Local college that has an aviation mechanics program just beginning and has a pilot training program in the planning stage
2 = Local community causes (Community charities, Homeless, etc.)
3 = Ecological causes (Recycling research; Air, water, and noise control, etc.)
4 = Political causes (Citizens for Better Government, Get-out-the-vote campaign, etc.)
5 = Health and family care issues (AIDS and/or other disease research, etc.)
6 = Animal causes (Save the whales, Save the Owls, Save the _____, etc.)
7 = Educational causes (Support for a primary or secondary school in your area, support for an aviation program at a local technical school, improving dropout rate in your area schools)
8 = Other issue or program that your team considers to be an important corporate social performance goal. This should be written on the margin of the decision form each quarter.
9 = General charitable causes, not specified

✔ While it would be difficult to ascertain a cost/benefit for this budget item, many firms believe strongly in supporting the communities in which they do business. The argument is made that a "strong community is good for our business in the long run."

DECISION 13: SELLING AND REDEEMING STOCK   (no commas) $_____

> Your company may choose to raise capital by issuing common stock. It is sold at the closing price posted the previous quarter and the funds are available immediately. To sell stock, enter the **dollar amount** (not the number of shares) on the decision form.

Explanation

The current market price is posted on your quarter-end financial statement and this is the price at which the stock will be sold. This sale will take place on the first day of the upcoming quarter so the cash from the sale is available in the quarter in which the stock is sold.

✔ If financial conditions warrant, your stock may be repurchased at market price anytime after quarter 5. However, your bank requires that you have no greater than a 1:4 equity-to-debt ratio at all times as a condition of your loans. That is, you should have *at least* $1 in equity for each $4 in loans (including long- and short-term loans). Maximum redemption is $500,000 per quarter.

✔ You may repurchase stock by placing a minus sign before the dollar amount you want to redeem; however, you may <u>never</u> have less than 150,000 shares.

✔ Your corporate charter requires that you maintain a minimum of 150,000 shares of stock (the beginning number of shares in quarter 0).

✔ Remember that the Earnings per Share figure is affected any time additional stock is issued. This is termed "dilution of stock value" but can be overcome with improved earnings in future quarters.

✔ If you give shares of stock to employees (Decision 6, Employee Compensation), the <u>number of shares of stock will increase</u> by the number required to make the stock-bonus payment.

DECISION 14: SHORT-TERM LOANS (Use minus sign to make a loan payment) $_____

> Your firm will need additional working capital as it grows. This is the purpose of short-term loans. Your line of credit is based on several financial factors.

Explanation

Short-term loans are based on a 90-day demand note. You may expect the bank to agree to renew (roll over) these notes every 90 days automatically if desired. However, during certain tight fiscal conditions, banks may call the demand note for payment. For this reason, firms should be very careful about borrowing long-term capital needs on a short-term (demand) note. Repayment of short-term notes is your responsibility, i.e., the loan will be automatically renewed unless you place the desired repayment amount on the decision form as a negative number. Your short-term interest rate will fluctuate with your firm's overall financial condition; it will be posted on your report each quarter.

The current short-term loan annual rate is 10%. The bank's requirement for the short-term loan is that it <u>may not be used for the purchase of aircraft</u>. This is the purpose of the long-term loans. Short-term loans are used for increasing working capital when increasing budgets.

DECISION 15: LONG-TERM LOANS (Enter minus for extra loan payoff) $_____

> Your airline may borrow long-term capital with long-term (mortgage) loans at 9% for the purchase of aircraft. This interest rate is fixed for the duration of the simulation. Your bank has granted your firm a line of credit, which includes both long-term and short-term loans. This line of credit is posted on your quarterly report.

Explanation

Place the amount of NEW loan desired. The bank will make an automatic deduction from cash for a loan payment. If you wish to make an additional loan payment in addition to the automatic payment, use a minus sign to make the additional repayment.

If you want to borrow more than the line of credit, you may do so by increasing your equity (i.e., selling stock). For each $1 in stock sold, the long-term loan limit increases $4. You may sell stock and borrow this larger amount in the same quarter.

The long-term loan is issued for approximately 12 years. Since you may be adding to this blanket mortgage loan from time to time, the repayment schedule could get complex; therefore, to simplify the repayment computation, 2% of the balance of the long-term loan is automatically deducted from your bank account each quarter. The bank will lend UP TO 80% of the value of an aircraft being purchased. Thus, you may borrow less than 80% of the price of an aircraft but not more. In any case, you will need to obtain the balance through the sale of stock or cash on hand.

An example on financing an aircraft:

Cost of Aircraft	$2,200,000
Sell Stock for 20% of the New Loan	−400,000
New Long-term Loan Required	$1,800,000

Note: *You must record the stock and loan values on the decision form. The program will not do your financing for you when you acquire a new aircraft.*

✔ If you want to make a new loan and pay off an old loan, enter the net value. For example, old loan balance = $500,000. New funds required: $750,000. Enter the difference, or $250,000.

✔ The bank will reduce your cash for an automatic loan repayment amounting to 2% of the loan balance each quarter.

Overdraft Loans

If your firm does not have a good method of cash planning, your cash position may be in jeopardy. Any time the cash outflow is greater than cash income, the bank will automatically issue an emergency loan for the exact amount of the overdraft and the loan is added to the short-term loan balance already in existence. The interest charged will be twice the usual short-term rate for the firm (20 to 22%) for one quarter. The rate then reverts to the short-term rate.

The interest is charged the first day of the FOLLOWING quarter. You can determine quickly if you have had an emergency loan issued because your cash balance will be zero! You are not required to make any decision form entry to pay off an overdraft loan, as it becomes part of your current short-term loan. You can pay all, part, or none of it whenever your cash position allows.

A Note on Interest Expenses

The total interest expense shown on the report will consist of Short-term loan interest + Previous Quarter's Overdraft loan interest + Long-term loan interest.

DECISION 16: DIVIDENDS PAID   (Total dollars to be paid) $_____

> The firm paid its shareholders $2,000 in dividends last quarter. A dividend payment may be adjusted by your accounting firm if the payment exceeds past profit, or if the dividend is too large for the cash position of the firm.

Explanation

In addition to a cash dividend, your firm may declare a 5% stock dividend. This grants 5% more shares to each shareholder without any direct cash cost to the firm. The number of shares outstanding will be adjusted on the firm's quarterly report. To enter this decision, place a "1" on the decision form in the

11

"Dividends Paid" block. If your firm declares an unusually large dividend at the end of the simulation, it will be construed as a stock price ploy and appropriate action will be taken with your game ranking score. If you have <u>negative retained earnings</u>, your dividend will be canceled. (Sorry, it's the law!)

✔ *It should be noted that the shareholders are the owners of the firm and do expect dividends as soon as possible.*

DECISION 17: PURCHASE 92 DAY CERTIFICATES OF DEPOSIT $_____

> If your firm grows and becomes profitable, it may have additional funds that should be invested in a Certificate of Deposit.

Explanation

Although some portion of your cash must be set aside for current expenses incurred but not yet paid (i.e., accounts payable), excess cash can be used to generate investment income. You may buy 92-day certificates of deposit that pay interest at 3% less than the prime lending rate (5% annual). These CD's expire on the first day of the coming quarter and <u>will not be available as cash in the quarter they are purchased.</u> They are NOT available for cash during the quarter in which they were purchased. Thus, if you have a cash flow problem, it is possible to need an (emergency) overdraft loan while owning a certificate of deposit.

✔ Another alternative for excess cash is to pay off any short-term and/or long-term loans. You should *not* finish the simulation with a large cash balance AND bank loan balances.

DECISIONS 18 to 23: ACQUISITION OF AIRCRAFT

> There are seven types of aircraft available to your company. Each has unique benefits and limitations (see Table 4 below). All of the aircraft are preowned but are in excellent condition. When you takeover the airline, it has three type A aircraft (19 seats each).

There are two sections on the decision form that can be used for aircraft acquisition. You may use one (Decision items 18 to 20) for leasing and the other (Decision items 21 to 23) for purchasing. Or you may acquire one type of aircraft on one section and another type of aircraft on the other section.

FIRST ACQUISITION TRANSACTION

18. Number of Aircraft (0 to 4)
19. Type of Aircraft (A to G) **See Table 4 for the key.**   _____
20. Lease(1) or Purchase(2) of this type aircraft   _____

    _____

SECOND ACQUISITION TRANSACTION

21. Number of Aircraft (0 to 4)
22. Type of Aircraft (A to G) **See Table 4 for the key.**   _____
23 Lease(1) or Purchase(2) of this type aircraft   _____

    _____

✔ Tip: Do not acquire large capacity aircraft (F – G) until you have built up customers in a market.

✔ If you want to acquire more than the program allows, you will need to do it next quarter. Sorry!

12

TABLE 4: AIRCRAFT SPECIFICATION DATA

KEY Name	Cost (millions)	Seats	Cruise MPH	Cabin Class	Type	Quarterly Lease	Notes
A = Beechcraft 1900	$2.0	19	268	No	Prop Jet	$80,000	No toilet, low headroom
B = British Aero 31	$2.2	18	253	Yes	Prop Jet	$82,000	Standing room, toilet
C = Embraer Brasilia	$3.1	30	294	Yes	Prop Jet	$132,000	Standing room, toilet
D = Saab 340	$3.4	34	272	Yes	Prop Jet	$144,000	Standing room, toilet
E = EmbraerERJ135	$4.3	37	400	Yes	Jet	$184,000	Standing room, toilet
F = ATR42	$4.4	46	300	Yes	Prop Jet	$185,000	Standing room, toilet
G = ERJ145RegionalJet or Embraer Jet	$5.8	50	450	Yes	Jet	$240,000	Standing room, toilet

Notes on Aircraft Acquisitions:

1. Because there is a sufficient number of manufacturers of commuter aircraft, delivery time is very short; you may order an aircraft for either purchase or lease and expect to put it into service on the first day of the next quarter (e.g., the quarter you are turning in the decision form). Used aircraft are also selling very well and you can expect to sell your used aircraft quickly, having the cash in the quarter in which they are sold.

2. The maximum number of aircraft a firm may have is 15.

3. Cabin class indicates enough headroom to walk upright in aisles, facilitating the ability to serve food and drinks. The type indicates if the aircraft is a prop jet (propellers powered by jet engines) or pure jet (Jet). Only the aircraft you are starting with are non-cabin class.

4. While there are several other manufacturers of commuter/regional aircraft, the types shown above are simply a sample of the sizes and features available. The lack of production in the U. S. of a given variety of commuter aircraft has provided an international look to many U.S. fleets. All aircraft listed above have very acceptable safety and maintenance records and there is no attempt in the simulation to offer one aircraft that is "better" than another.

5. The key to aircraft selection is in matching equipment to the market. The optimum (round trip) range for types A, B, and C is 280 - 400 miles, and types D, E, F, and G are optimum for flights at and above 400 miles. This does not mean that you can't use aircraft above or below their optimum mileage but the costs will be slightly higher if you do.

➜ ➜ **REMINDER: Make the Necessary Financial Arrangements to Acquire Aircraft.**

Aircraft can be either purchased or leased. If purchased, aircraft can be financed through loans, issuing stock, or a combination of both. If leased, the lease is a ten year operating lease. An operating lease requires no current financial outlay but the aircraft reverts to the lessor at the end of the lease. Your present fleet is financed through a combination of debt and equity; their values and accumulated depreciation are reflected on the BALANCE SHEET and on the FLEET STATUS REPORT.

✔ Types C to G must be used for luxury service. For clarity, any priced airline may own these type aircraft. **Type A must not be used in luxury service.** Type B could be used but customer satisfaction would be very poor.

✔ Do not forget to sell stock or take a loan to *purchase* an aircraft. The program does not do this for you automatically!

13

DECISIONS 24 to 26: DISPOSAL OF AIRCRAFT

> You may dispose of up to three aircraft in a quarter. Leased or owned aircraft may be disposed. The cost to dispose of a leased aircraft is $50,000. An owned aircraft will be sold at book value (cost less accumulated depreciation). A brokerage fee of 2% of the book value of the aircraft will be assessed. The disposal costs will be shown as "Other Expenses" on the Income and Expense statement. Due to space limitations on the decision form, you can only dispose of three aircraft each quarter.

✔ *Use the SERIAL NUMBER of the aircraft and not the aircraft type. The serial numbers are at the top of page 2 on the report.*

24. **Serial Number of one aircraft to be sold** _____ (Use this slot first)
25. **Serial Number of one aircraft to be sold** _____ (Use this slot second)
26. **Serial Number of one aircraft to be sold** _____

✔ Once you have disposed of an aircraft, DO NOT place it on the next quarter's decision form!

✔ Enter zeros if you do not have any aircraft sales. Sorry, but only 3 disposals at a time!

Other Factors in Disposing of Aircraft

Although it is somewhat costly to dispose of an aircraft that your firm has purchased or leased, you should do so if the aircraft no longer fits your strategy. If you want to convert a leased aircraft to a purchase, talk with your instructor and he/she may refund the $50,000 charge through the "Other Expense Adjustment" feature in the Compute section of the program. (Some instructors do not as it is a chore on their part.)

DECISION 27: MARKET RESEARCH STUDIES   (0 to $31000; no comma) $_____

> Most of the market research activity in the airline industry involves counting passengers and reading timetables. However, there are certain studies that can be useful for planning purposes. You may purchase any or all of the following reports:

● Business conditions forecast for four quarters $1,000

● Average industry quality budget and the employee compensation plan for each airline $2,000

● Estimate of average fare for each airline and the cabin service policy for each airline $4,000

● The estimate of <u>total</u> seats sold daily in each market (not the seats for each company) $8,000
   This is printed on page 3 of your report in the second column.

● Average promotion and advertising budget, cargo airlines, and salespeople for each airline $16,000

To order market research reports, place the TOTAL AMOUNT for all studies desired on the decision form. For example, if you want the first two studies, you would enter $3,000 on the decision form ($1,000 + $2,000 but with no commas = 2000). All 5 studies would cost $31,000. In addition, you will be provided (at no charge) the current number of flights in each market for each competitor and the fare, sale, if any. These reports will be printed on page two of your firm's financial report.

✔ **Most teams do not order enough market research to keep informed about competitors.**

DECISION 28: INCIDENT RESPONSE

> Each quarter has a mini-case, which is termed an *incident*. These may be found in Section 4. Your team will need to debate the issues being presented by the incident and enter the appropriate response here. If you don't like any of the choices, you must still select the one closest to your opinion. The incidents are required, not optional.

Explanation

The response to the decisions may or may not have an effect on your firm's sales or costs in subsequent quarters. USE INCIDENT A FOR QUARTER 1 (your first decision) which is creating the name for your company. Thereafter, the incident to use will be listed in the MESSAGES section on your quarterly report.

VERIFICATION TOTAL>>>>>>>>>>

The Verification Total has no impact on your results, but helps the person entering the decisions. If the total on the decision routine matches the total items on the decision form, the values have been entered correctly. Add all positive values and subtract any negative values.

DECISION 29: CHANGES IN MARKETS SERVED

> Your overall strategy will be reflected in your decisions regarding which markets to serve, and how many flights to schedule with which size aircraft. Refer to the market entry section below (Table 5) as you read through this section.

Only enter values for a market you want to change! For example, you do not need to enter a market that you served the previous quarter unless you are making a change in one of the elements in that market. You may enter changes up to a maximum of 14 markets.

You may "mix" the types of aircraft serving a market. Enter the total seats representing this mix. Examples are shown below in Table 5.

To abandon a market, enter the market number and all zeros.

✔ If you are changing any items in a currently held market, <u>enter all items</u> even though you may be changing only one item this quarter.

✔ You do not need to enter a market that you served the previous quarter unless you are making a change in one of the elements in that market.

TABLE 5
MARKET CHANGES
REPRODUCTION OF DECISION FORM PAGE
(These are not quarter 0 entries but sample entries.)

Market Number	Round trip Flights Per Day		Total Seats Per Day (Flights x Seats on A/C)	Type of Fare Sale (0 – 3)	Notes
1	3	(3 x 19) =	57	0	Served by 19-seat Beechcraft
2	2	(2 x 19) =	38	1	Served by 19-seat Beechcraft; Promo fare 1
3	3	(2 x 19+1 x 30) =	68	2	2 flts w/Beechcraft, 1 Metroliner; Promo fare 2
7	1	(1 x 30) =	30	2	Brasilia serving a resort market; resorts must have a fare sale of 2 or 3.
6	4	(4 x 18) =	72	0	4 flts w/Jetstream
5	0		0	0	Abandoning this market. **Note: You must zero out a market to abandon it**

The entry form contains blanks for 14 market changes. You may make more the next quarter! This is done to protect your firm the added expense and stress of too many changes at one time.

INSTRUCTIONS FOR ENTERING MARKET CHANGES

✔ All fare sales revert to zero after one quarter <u>with the exception of Resort flights</u>, which will stay at fare sale 2. This will keep you from entering fare sale on resort markets ea ch period.

✔ Flights are always entered as the number of Round trip flights between the cities comprising the market. You should take this into consideration when calculating the mileage involved.

✔ NEVER schedule less than two round trip flights per day except in resort and foreign markets where one flight per day is acceptable, but not necessarily optimum.

✔ Double check your TOTAL SEATS PER DAY in each market. This number must not exceed the formula shown (# flights x seats on the type aircraft flown) because you will be charged operating costs based on the total seats in each market.

✔ Enter zeros beside a market you wish to abandon. If a market is abandoned, and then re-entered later, it will take the usual three quarters to build up demand in the market.

✔ **A FINAL REMINDER!** To keep from entering all markets each quarter, enter only values for a market you want to change.

How to Complete the <u>Fare sale</u> Column

<u>Entry:</u>
- 0   Regular fare: No sales this quarter; usually used in developed markets.
- 1   One-month fare sale: 1/3 off the regular fare for one month. The next two months the fare would be the normal rate. Used when opening new markets and/or a short term sale.
- 2   Two-month fare sale: 1/3 off the regular fare for two months and then reverts to the regular fare for the third month. This fare is usually a breakeven fare, at best. Don't use extensively.
- 3   Three-month fare sale: 1/3 off the regular fare for all three months of the quarter. <u>This fare, while attracting the budget passenger will create a monetary loss in the market.</u>

✔ **Reminder: <u>All fare sales with the exception of resort fares will revert to zero after one quarter.</u>**

MARKETS SERVED

> **Before making any decisions, you MUST obtain from your instructor the number of teams that are playing the simulation.**

The simulation automatically creates a certain number of markets according to the number of teams competing. Table 6 indicates the market numbers used for various size classes (e.g., teams). Example: If 8 teams are competing, there would be a total of 35 markets available, consisting of market numbers 1 through 35.

TABLE 6
NUMBER OF MARKETS VERSUS NUMBER OF TEAMS

No. of Teams Participating	Market Numbers Used	No. of Teams Participating	Market Numbers Used
4	1 - 17	9	1 - 41
5	1 - 26	10	1 - 44
6	1 - 26	11	1 - 52
7	1 - 35	12	1 - 52
8	1 - 35		

Your firm is currently serving the cities (i.e., markets) as shown in Table 9 on page 19. Each firm in the simulation begins with the same general market structure and exactly the same passenger load (i.e., sales). Each firm is competing with one or two other firms in four markets and each has a market that currently has no other carrier in it. There are also markets that have just had a major carrier pull out and are therefore now open to the commuter airlines in the simulation. Routes range in length up to 600 round trip miles with an average daily passenger load between 15 and 32 passengers. In addition to the regular routes, there are one or more resort markets that are 600 miles and currently have an estimated demand of 18 to 22 passengers per day. Currently no firm is serving this market.

Seven Different Types of Markets

These different configurations are included in Table 7. Each market is identified with an Identification Letter (A, B, C, D, E, F, R). In order to accommodate a different number of teams, several markets in the table below have identical characteristics. You can find the markets that your airline is now serving and the total market structure for your size industry by consulting the following tables.

Your firm is currently serving one Market Type A, one Market Type B, one Market type C, one Market Type D, and one Market Type E. No one is serving any markets represented by Market Types F (a foreign market) or R (a resort market).

Opening New Markets

Your team may add **any market in the simulation** *at any time*. The cost to open a new market is $10,000. This cost is automatically charged to <u>Passenger Service expenses</u>. The new market is opened immediately. There is no waiting period. Your team may also abandon a market at any time at no cost.

TABLE 7
MARKET CHARACTERISTICS

Market Type	Market Number	Beginning Demand Per Firm R-T Seats Per Day	Round-Trip Miles	Description
A	1,9,21,30,38 47	15	600	From your mini-hub to a medium city with light manufacturing and service businesses.
B	2,10,22,31, 39,48	27	400	Service between 2 medium cities. One has a large number of service businesses and the other a military base.
C	3,11,23,32, 40,49	15	340	From your mini-hub to a regional hub that has a large number of heavy manufacturing firms.
D	4,12,24,33, 41,50	27	360	From your mini-hub to a medium city that has a major university and extensive business services, with a stopover halfway out from the hub at small but growing technology cluster. For simplicity, fares are the same to either destination.
E	5,7,13,15,18, 25,27,34,36, 42,45,51	36	400	From your mini-hub to a medium city that has a new and growing industrial park.
F	6,8,14,16,19, 26,28,35,37, 43,46,52	30 to 60	420	From your mini-hub to a foreign city not too far from the border that has a diversified industry and tourist trade. See Note 2 below.
R	17,20,29,44	20 to 30	600	From your mini-hub to major resort/recreation area like Las Vegas; Vail, Col.;Orlando, Fla.; Atlantic City, N.J. See Note 3 below.

Notes:

1. Market type indicates that these markets have similar demand.

2. This is the opportunity to become an international carrier. Depending on your operating area, the foreign city could be one of the following. Any cabin class aircraft would be ideal for the route **but the 19-seat A/C, Type A should not be used.**

> Canada: Halifax, Montreal, Quebec, Toronto, Winnipeg, Vancouver
> Mexico: Tijuana, Mexicali, Hermosillo, Chihuahua, Juarez
> Bahamas: Freeport, Nassau, and various out islands

3. Cabin Class aircraft (Types B – G) and a fare sale #2 or #3 fare must be utilized in the resort market (Type R). While no airline is flying there now, it is thought the demand can be developed. Even if there are no competitors in the resort market, there are charter flights by tour operators that keep the price pressure heavy; thus the required fare sale of 2 or 3.

Use Table 8 below to obtain the markets your firm is in. Then go back to Table 7 to ascertain the TYPE of market for each.

TABLE 8
MARKETS SERVED BY EACH COMPANY AT THE BEGINNING
OF THE SIMULATION (Quarter 0)

Co. #	Competitive Market # Served	Your Market With no Competition	The Closest Foreign Market no One is Serving	The Closest Resort Market no One is Serving
1	1,2,3,4	5	6	17
2	1,2,3,4	7	8	17
3	9,10,11,12	13	14	17
4	9,10,11,12	15	16	17
5	21,22,23,24	18	19	20
6	21,22,23,24	25	26	20
7	30,31,32,33	27	28	29
8	30,31,32,33	34	35	29
9	38,39,40,41	36	37	29
10	38,39,40,41	42	43	44
11	47,48,49,50	45	46	44
12	47,48,49,50	51	52	44

Check the market characteristics (Table 7) to determine the characteristics of each market you are in. Then complete the chart on the next page to ascertain the size and characteristics of your current markets. The example below is for Company 8. Note that the market numbers are copied (left to right) from Table 8, in the order given, onto the appropriate blanks in Chart 1.

TABLE 9
EXAMPLE OF MARKETS SERVED FOR COMPANY 8

Market #	Market Type	Round trip Flights/day	Total Seats Avail/day	Estimate of Seats Sold per day
30	A	2	38	18
31	B	3	57	30
32	C	2	38	18
33	D	3	57	30
34	E	3	57	45
35	F	0	0	0
29	R	0	0	0

Complete the following chart using market numbers from Table 8.

Chart 1
Your Airline's Beginning Markets

	Market #	Market Type	Round trip Flights/day	Total Seats Avail/day
	__	A	2	38
Fill in the >>>>>>>>>>	__	B	3	57
Market Numbers >>>>	__	C	2	38
in the slots >>>>>>>>>	__	D	3	57
using Table 8 >>>>>>>	__	E	3	57
on previous page>>>>>	__	F	0	0
This is your starting markets	__	R	0	0

The following formula shows how to calculate number of seats that you make <u>available</u> per day:
Round trips x Capacity of the Aircraft flying this route = Seats Available (e.g., 3 x 19 = 57)

MARKETS IN WHICH YOUR FIRM MAY COMPETE

In the first quarter of the simulation, in addition to your current markets, *you may begin service in ANY MARKET IN THE SIMULATION*. Thus, if you are company #7 in a seven company industry, you may start service in any market in your industry (Market #1 through #29 - see Table 8). If you are company #4 in an 11 company industry, you may enter any market in that size industry (market #1 through #46). At the beginning of the simulation, each company is serving a market by itself (a no-competition market); this is not a monopoly! Other teams may enter this market at any time.

✔ **Note: Use the Aircraft Scheduling Worksheet (Form 5) in the back of this manual to calculate number of seats, markets, and allowable mileage each quarter. There is a substantial penalty if you exceed <u>either your number of seats or your allowable mileage.</u>**

To help you visualize the route system in the simulation, a generic route map is shown on the next page.

FARE SALES

The last column of the "Changes in Markets Served" section on the decision form allow you to have special fare sales for one to three months. Fare sales are used to promote your airline in a new market <u>but should never be used on an on-going basis due to the loss of revenues they create.</u> More on page 24.

Decision
Form Entry:
0. Regular Fare
1. One-month sale = one-third off the regular fare for 1 month. The next two months would be at the normal fare.
2. Two-month sale = one-third off the regular fare for two months and then revert to the regular fare for the third month. The constant use of fare sale 2 is not profitable in the long run!
3. Three-month sale = one-third off the regular fare for all three months of the quarter.

✔ <u>**All fare sales with the exception of resort fares will revert to zero after one quarter.**</u>

✔ **Resort fare sales stay at the sale established.** Warning: A fare sale of 3 in a resort market will create a loss situation.

CONFUSED? HERE ARE SUGGESTIONS FOR QUARTER 1 TO GET YOU STARTED.
(A student contribution)

1. Choose an aircraft to acquire from 30 to 37 seats. (That is large enough to cover the longer routes). You can always change your fleet later. Lease it and you won't have to worry with financing this quarter.
2. Choose markets to fly to. Add a flight to your Type C market (340 miles), 3 flights to your competitor's monopoly market (after all, there is enough business for everyone!), and 1 flight to you're a market (600 miles). That totals 1740 out of the 1800 miles allotted to a new aircraft. Later, you may want to pull your 19 seat aircraft from that 600 mile market and place a more appropriate aircraft there.
3. Leave your fare at .35 or .36 until you see what the competition is going to do.
4. Increase your advertising and promotion to support your new market activities.
5. That's it. It is NOT an optimal strategy but one which beats nothing! The writer assumes no liability for this strictly "short-term" strategy!

GENERIC ROUTE MAP FOR ALL FIRMS

This generic route map is shown to aid you in visualizing the markets and their relationships. It is termed *generic* because this two hub route scheme repeats according to the number of firms competing in a class (for every two firms there is a pair of hubs as shown below). To match up your markets to this map, use Tables 7, 8, and Chart 1. At the beginning of the simulation, all firms are competing with other firms in a market represented by Market Types A, B, C, and D. All firms are operating without competition in one market represented by Type E. No one is serving markets in Market Types F (foreign) or R (resort).

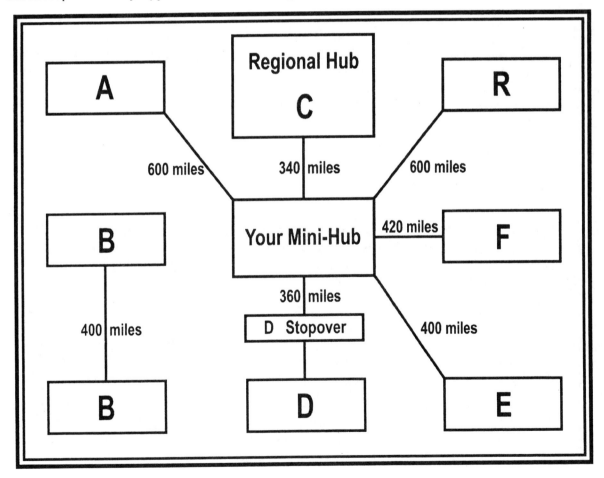

```
┌─────────────────────────────────────────────┐
│                  SECTION 2                    │
│             DECISION INFORMATION              │
└─────────────────────────────────────────────┘
```

> If you have information overload at this point, you may skip this section until after you
> have made your first decisions. However it *must* be read after you have received the first
> decision's report. It will aid in *"polishing up"* your strategy.

AIRCRAFT UTILIZATION AND SCHEDULING

Airplanes do not generate revenues when they sit on the ground. Therefore, utilization is a variable that
can affect successful operations. A typical aircraft will be scheduled from 12 to 14 hours per day and
during that time can fly 1,800 miles per day. This will allow overnight maintenance and 8 to 12 legs per
day. Overuse of aircraft will lead to *costly mechanical failure*. The quarterly report your team receives
will contain the mileage flown during the quarter and the MAXIMUM mileage allowed. The maximum
mileage is calculated by how many miles the average commuter aircraft can fly in the normal 12 - 14 hour
flight day:

1800 miles per day x 80 flight days per quarter = 144,000 miles per aircraft per quarter.

✔ **Use the Scheduling Form on page 102 to ensure that you are optimizing your available mileage.**

If you exceed the maximum, you may expect additional maintenance costs and "DOWNTIME," with the
accompanying loss of passengers as flight schedules are canceled. A form, "Aircraft Scheduling
Worksheet" is included in the back of this manual for you to calculate the mileage each quarter. A small
amount of additional mileage will be accommodated to allow for minor mathematical errors on your part.
While there may be a slight decrease in maintenance costs if you fly less than 100% of the maximum
miles allowed, it is also good strategy to fly the maximum miles in order to more completely utilize your
fleet.

The maximum mileage is calculated on a fleet basis; therefore, if the total mileage scheduled is somewhat
less than the maximum, you may be able to squeeze out one more flight. You must fly this flight in the
aircraft with the lowest number of flight miles. In other words, you could not fly the extra flight with a
preferred aircraft.

Your takeover fleet of three Beech 1900s is serving several markets. Cabin service is not provided; it is
not practical on this type of aircraft, as it does not have enough headroom for stand-up serving. The major
advantage is that by having a bullet-shaped fuselage, it has a higher cruise speed than most of its
competitors. This aircraft MUST NOT BE USED IN LUXURY SERVICE.

The 18-passenger Jetstream does have the headroom for food and beverage service; however, it costs
more and has one less seat than the Metroliner. Since the FAA does not require a cabin attendant for
aircraft of less than 30 seats, placing a cabin attendant on this aircraft just to provide cabin service would
be uneconomical. Firms should attempt to match markets, demand, and amenities with the type of aircraft
placed into service.

While the current fleet of 19-passenger aircraft is serving the airline at the present time, increased demand
will place a strain on your fleet. While the current fare of 35 cents per passenger mile has been generating
enough revenue for the current fleet, the higher costs of purchasing or leasing added planes may require
a somewhat higher fare structure. If you do raise fares, it is suggested that you increase fares slowly (1
cent per mile) and determine how the increase affects your demand and what reaction it has on your
competitors' pricing.

22

Market Success Factors

The number of flights per day is a crucial factor to the success of an airline. Too few flights prompt prospective passengers to drive to the nearest competing hub and too many can be too costly to maintain. With the exception of the resort run, it is not practical to fly only one or two round-trip flights per day into a market; there would be no passenger loyalty and the cost to maintain a station there would be prohibitive. Since the breakeven point for a flight is 45% to 55% load, the careful balancing of flights and seats in a market is an important decision for your team.

When entering a market for the first time, your management team should recognize that there is a certain "lag" effect of developing that market. Advertising and sales promotion will be an important part of developing new markets. It may take one or more quarters to fully develop a market.

You can differentiate yourself in individual markets by your frequency of service (flights per day in a given market), seats flown per day in that market, aircraft choice for that route, and fare sales (when desired). Three or more round trip flights per day in a market is usual while two round trip flights is minimally acceptable. Therefore, you may NEVER schedule less than two flights per day. The exception to this is the resort area and foreign market (F); you may serve these markets with one flight per day.

This is a "market driven" industry and simulation. It is VERY IMPORTANT to continually analyze markets, calculate breakeven number of passengers, and make adjustments. Customers are NOT very brand loyal and look for attributes such as frequency of service (which also translates into number of seats provided in a market per day), and, to a lesser extent, price of the fare. Costs are relatively fixed in the airline business (e.g., it costs nearly the same amount to transport one or nineteen passengers between two points). Sometimes the difference between a profit and loss is one additional passenger per flight per day!

✔ **It takes two to three quarters to develop a new market and build a passenger base.**

Mix and Match Aircraft Types

Most manufacturers advertise that the breakeven load for their aircraft is in the 45% to 55% range; this covers all operating costs but not fixed costs. You may mix the type of aircraft serving a market. For example, you may schedule two flights of a type A aircraft (19 seats) and two flights of a type C aircraft (30 seats) for a total of four daily flights and 98 daily seats in market number X (19+19+30+30).

The Computer Program Optimizes Your Aircraft Scheduling

The program will optimize your daily aircraft scheduling For example, if you have three flights with the same type aircraft, it will assign departure times of 7 a.m., 1 p.m., and 7 p.m. If you have four flights, with two small aircraft and two larger aircraft, the departure times for the larger aircraft would be 7 a.m. and 7 p.m. The smaller aircraft would depart at 11 a.m. and 3 p.m. This scheduling assumption is based on the fact that loads are larger for the first morning flight and the last evening flight.

MARKET REGIONS AND ADDITIONAL COSTS

Due to longer distances involved when a firm operates out of its usual geographic region, there may be slight additional costs of serving those markets outside your current region. These costs are for overnight expenses for the crew, maintenance runs to airports without maintenance facilities, and purchasing fuel at the destination regardless of price at that location. Thus, direct flight expenses may be *slightly* higher for markets served outside your region. While the additional expense is not prohibitive, you should be aware of the possibility.

As the length of the flight increases (termed "stage"length), the average seat mile cost declines; thus it is more efficient to operate aircraft over longer stage lengths. However, to simplify the financial report, all of these factors are taken into consideration and an average cost per seat mile is calculated. Each firm's region is assumed to be those markets shown on Table 8 beside each firm's company number.

FARE SALES

The following list indicates the sales on fares that are available and what their effect would be on the ticket price for a 400-mile flight.

Decision
Form Entry:
  0. Regular Fare .35 per mile × 400 miles = $140.00 ticket revenue
  1. One-month sale = 1/3 off the regular fare for 1 month. The next two months the fare would be the normal $140.00. Average ticket revenue $124.44.
  2. Two-month sale = 1/3 off the regular fare for two months and then revert to the regular fare for the third month. Average ticket revenue $108.92.
  3. Three-month sale = 1/3 off the regular fare for all three months of the quarter. Average ticket revenue $93.33.

✔ Teams should be very aware of the large losses that will occur if the sale on fares is used in all markets in the same quarter.

The following tabulation describes the effect on revenues in a market when the various sale pricing strategies are involved. Be aware of the losses that occur when having a sale of two or three months (with the exception of resort markets, where additional demand helps to make up for the fare sale of 2).

	Revenues Lost	Net Revenues
1-month sale on fares	11%	89%
2-month sale on fares	22%	78%
3-month sale of fares	33%	67%

DEMAND

Overall demand is affected by several factors, including general business conditions, availability of flights, fare structures, the optimism of the traveling public about economic conditions, and whether vacation plans via air are in order. In addition, the demand includes the growth of the regional airline business, as larger carriers pull out of unprofitable markets. A news message will be printed on your quarterly report announcing various types of economic activity in certain markets; this may necessitate adding flights or beginning service in these markets. Analyzing your existing and potential markets is a key element in managing your airline.

A current demand index is printed at the top of the second page of the student report and is based on a starting index of 100. Future forecasts of demand may be obtained by purchasing the first Market Research Study ($1,000). Remember that a forecast is *just a forecast*, not a certainty. The demand forecasts are updated each quarter and a new four-quarter forecast made. Do not assume you can purchase a demand forecast every four quarters and have up-to-date information!

If the current demand is 100 and forecasted demand the next quarter is 110, this would indicate a 10% increase in overall industry demand. If additional flights are added to a market, there can be some demand stimulated as travelers switch from ground to air transportation. For quarter one planning, the demand forecast is very positive-a 5% to 10% increase in demand in each of the next two quarters.

OTHER COSTS

Refunds and Your Reliability Factor

Refunds must be made when passengers are not able to fly as a result of equipment problems, weather, overbooking, incorrect ticketing, employee discourtesy, or baggage problems. This airline has a reliability factor of about 91%, which means that about 9% of its flights are affected in some manner. The reliability for the quarter will be printed beside the REFUND column on the Income statement. Next is an example of the method of calculation: 100 − reliability x gross income, e.g., 100− 1.58 = 8.42.

✔ The winter quarter is particularly difficult to keep an airline on schedule; you may expect your usual reliability to be reduced about 2 to 4% during the winter quarter (Quarters 4, 8, and 12).

Commissions

Commissions paid to travel agents are 10% of the ticket price; however, not all tickets are sold through agents so the commission expense will be calculated at about 9% of the gross revenues at the beginning of the simulation.

Direct Flight Expenses

Flight operation, fuel, maintenance, and passenger service expenses are directly related to miles flown. The current cost for these four items is about 12 to 13 cents per seat mile flown. Thus, for the 19-passenger Beech 1900 this would be (.12 x 19 seats) $2.28 per mile flown. The 30-seat Brasilia would cost about $3.60 per mile flown (.12 x 30 seats). These four key items are distributed as follows at the beginning of the simulation:

	Cents per Seat Mile	% of Total
Flight Operations	3.60	30%
Fuel	2.88	23%
Maintenance	3.12	27%
Passenger Service	2.40	20%
	12.00¢	100%

Flight operations include crew cost, dispatching and weather services, baggage/mail/cargo handling, and aircraft handling on the ground. Passenger service includes the cost of the reservation and ticketing service, ticket counters and terminal baggage service, and rent of terminal passenger areas. The $10,000 cost associated with opening a new market is added to passenger service expenses. Cabin (food) service is not included in the above costs. It is shown separately on the income and expense statement.

Insurance

Insurance costs are based on the total seats in the fleet and the size of the aircraft. The current cost of $10,260 is based on the following calculation: 3 aircraft with 19 seats each = 57 seats x $180 per seat per quarter = $10,260. Larger-capacity aircraft have a higher insurance rate. Any aircraft in the fleet with more than 20-seat capacity are charged $300 per seat per quarter.

Employee Turnover Cost

The total cost of replacing an employee due to turnover is $3,000. This amount includes the cost of termination of the former employee; selection, interviewing, and hiring costs; on-the-job-training (OJT) costs; and the cost of lower productivity by the new employee during the early quarters of employment. Three factors will affect employee turnover: additional employee compensation, training, and reliability.

Depreciation

Depreciation is calculated at 1.75% of the cost of each aircraft <u>owned</u> per quarter. This seemingly low rate takes into account the salvage (resale) value of the aircraft at the end of any given number of years of use. In addition, the facilities and equipment account is depreciated at $5,000 per quarter.

Taxes

Taxes are calculated at 40% of profits. If a firm has losses, the tax credit will carry forward in the amount of the losses. Therefore, a quarter in which you use up all your tax credits may show less tax expense than usual, as the 40% rate will apply to the nonsheltered profits only. While the 40% rate may appear high, it includes not only income taxes, but property tax, licenses, and VAT in the areas where that tax is in effect.

Administrative Expense (Overhead)

Administrative expense is a variable amount based on the total number of seats in your fleet. While these costs may be changed by the game administrator, the cost at the beginning of the simulation is as follows:

Number of Seats	Administrative Cost Per Quarter	
0-76	$100,000	
77-102	$150,000	
103-134	$200,000	
135-168	$250,000	
169-199	$300,000	
200-230	$350,000	
231-279	$400,000	
>279	$450,000	plus $1,700 per seat over 280

The increases in cost at various levels of fleet size are the result of extra management, support personnel, administrative space, and maintenance facilities required. <u>To repeat, this table lists the costs at the beginning of the simulation (quarter 1)</u>. Higher administrative costs may be incurred without warning as fleets and firms become larger or as non-controllable costs (airport gate rental costs, additional FAA reporting requirements, and airport security are examples).

Other Expenses

Other expense refers to expenditures that may occur from time to time but do not fit into other categories. This includes the brokerage fee when selling an aircraft or the fee to break a lease and other costs associated with the mini-cases or incidents described later in the manual.

✔ There could be more than one item making up the other expense total, so try to figure it out on your own before asking your instructor why the computer made an error!

This section contains an analysis of the quarter 0 financial statements WHICH IS THE STARTING FINANCIAL CONDITION OF YOUR FIRM. You will be taking over the airline at the beginning of quarter 1. The report you will receive each quarter will consist of a balance sheet, income and expense statement, cash flow analysis, operating data, and other industry information.

FINANCIAL REPORT OF STARTING POSITION

A report for your starting position (quarter 0) is shown on the next three pages. This is the "starting point" for your management team, that is, the current condition of the firm you are taking over. This is the same format for the report you will receive as feedback after each quarter.

You are purposely not given a large quantity of past performance data because the simulation represents a "new beginning" for this airline. Major carriers are pulling out of markets and changing their markets served daily, thus presenting new opportunities the firm has never had in the past.

The Balance Sheet

The balance sheet will indicate the usual balance sheet items. The net amount of the fixed asset "facilities and equipment" will be shown AFTER depreciation of $5,000 is deducted each quarter. (This is done to save space on the report.) Total Assets should be equal to Total Liabilities & Equity; however, due to rounding errors the two totals may be off slightly.

Cash Flow Analysis

This analysis will show the various cash sources and uses for the quarter. In the interest of space, some items are combined (e.g., commissions and refunds). Note that depreciation is subtracted from "Total Expenses" before it is entered on the cash flow analysis. This is due to the fact that depreciation is basically an accounting entry for tax purposes and not a cash expense at the time.

Market Research Report

This report will show the number of seats furnished in each market by each airline. If you purchase the $8,000 market research study, you will be furnished with the total number of seats sold in each market.

Fleet Status Report and News Messages

This report will show your current fleet of aircraft and information on their value, if purchased, or the lease cost, if leased. Other data included will be various news messages to your firm, and reports concerning your incident decisions.

Industry A	Quarterly Report	Quarter 0	Company X

** INCOME STATEMENT **

Gross Revenue	1,490,761
+ Interest Income	0
- Commissions	135,659
- Refunds (Reliability=92.0)	119,260
Net Revenue	1,235,842

Expenses:

Flight Operations	293,299
Fuel	225,253
Maintenance	254,192
Passenger Service	195,532
Cabin Service	0
Insurance	10,260
Marketing Expenses	5,000
Add. Employee Compensation	0
Quality and Training	1,000
Hiring/On-Job-Training Costs	24,000
Social Performance Budget	0
Market Research Cost	31,000
Interest Expense	10,364
Lease Payment	0
Administrative Exp	100,000
Depreciation	48,750
Other Expense	0
Total Operating Expense	1,195,650
Operating Profit/Loss	40,192
Other Profit/Loss	0
Cargo Profit less Marketing	0
Profit Before Tax	40,192
Less	
Total Taxes (40%)	16,076
Net Profit	24,116
Dividends Paid	2,000
Profits Retained	22,116

** CASH FLOW ANALYSIS **

Beginning Cash & Previous	91,640
Short-term Investment	0
Gross Revenue (60%)	+ 894,456
Accounts Receivable	+ 427,018
Stock Sold	+ 0
Loan Proceeds	+ 0
Other Inc & A/C Sale	+ 0
Total Cash Inflow	1,462,488
Commissions + Refunds	- 254,919
70% of Operating Ex	- 802,830
Accounts Payable	- 245,803
Taxes	- 16,076
Total Loan Payments	- 6,000
Purchase S-T Invest	- 0
Dividends	- 2,000
Equipment Purchase	- 0
Net Cash	34,861
Overdraft Loan	0
Ending Cash	85,785

** BALANCE SHEET **

Cash	85,785
Short-TERM Investment	0
Accounts Receivable	596,304
Total Current Assets	682,089

AIRCRAFT:

Cost	2,500,000
Less Depreciation	-800,000
Net Aircraft	1,700,000
Facilities/equip- net	+100,000
Fixed Assets	1,800,000
Total Assets	2,482,089

Accounts Payable	344,070
Short-term Loans	+150,000
Total Current Liabilities	494,070
Long-term Loans	300,000
Total Liabilities	794,070
Common Stock	1,500,000
Retained Earnings	188,019
Total Equity	1,688,019
Total Liabilities & Equity	2,482,089

** OTHER DATA **

Stock Price: per share	$20.00
Demand Index this Quarter	100
Total Aircraft/Seats	3/57
Total Revenue Passengers	20461
Total Miles Flown	428,800
Maximum Mileage	432,000
Available Seat Miles (a)	8,147,200
Revenue Passenger Miles (b)	4,259,321
Passenger Load Factor (b/a)	52.2%
Yield per Rev Pass Mile	$0.350
Yield per Avail Seat Mile (a)	$0.183
Cost per Avail Seat Mile (b)	$0.178
Profit per Avail Seat Mi (a-b)	$0.005
Total Employees	81
Employee Resignations (8.64%)	7
Fuel: Spot Price this quarter	$.96
Fuel: Contract next quarter	$.96
Line of Credit	$5,958,006
Short-term Int Rate	10.0%
Long-term Interest Rate	9.0%
Shares Stock Outstanding	150,000
Earnings per share	$ .15

28

*** FLEET STATUS REPORT ***

Aircraft Serial Number	A/C Type	Cost	Accumulated Depreciation	Book Value	Lease Cost $ per quarter
1	A	700,000	200,000	500,000	0
2	A	800,000	250,000	550,000	0
3	A	1,000,000	350,000	650,000	0

*** MARKET RESEARCH STUDIES ***

Smith Econometrics, Ltd. demand forecast for next 4 quarters:
        100 104 1XX 1XX

Employee Compensation Co. 1 to 4: 0/0   0/0   0/0   0/0
(First item is Compensation # and second item is the percent of wage increase)

Average Quality and Training Budget: $1,000

Fare for each company: .35   .35   .35   .35

Cabin Service Codes: 0   0   0   0

Average Promotion Budget: $2,500

Average Advertising Budget: $2,500

Average Quality Score is: 68

Salespersons for Co 1 to 4: 0   0   0   0

Firms in the Cargo Business: No firms are currently in the cargo business

Market research for Seats Sold is shown on page 3, column 2 of this report under the column titled "Total Sold"

*** NEWS MESSAGE TO YOUR FIRM INCLUDING INCIDENT FEEDBACK ***

Use Incident A in quarter 1 (Name your airline).
Note: It is normal to have low profits (or losses) when developing new markets.
Some markets are under served for the population base.
Congratulations to the new management team selected to operate this up-and-coming airline!

The overall demand for the next two quarters looks very promising for commuter/regional carriers due to the major airlines pulling out of many markets.

*** INDUSTRY DATA ***

Stock Prices for Co. 1 to 4: $20 $20 $20 $20

Total Aircraft and Seats for each company:
3/57   3/57   3/57   3/57

*** INDUSTRY FINANCIAL RATIOS ***

Current Ratio	Return on Sales	Return on Equity	Return on Assets	Debt to Equity	Daily Seat Productivity	Yield per Available Seat Mile
1.38	.009	.014	.009	.278	4.537	.183

Demand Index 100   ***Sales Report - Quarter 0 ***   Company 1

Format: Co#/Flights flown per day/Seats offered per day/Fare Sale/Seats Sold

Market Number	Total Seats Sold		
1	40	1/2/38/0/20	2/2/38/0/20
2	60	1/3/57/0/30	2/3/57/0/30
3	38	1/2/38/0/19	2/2/38/0/19
4	58	1/3/57/0/29	2/3/57/0/29
5	29	1/3/57/0/29	
6	29		2/3/57/0/29
7	29	2/3/57/0/29	
8	0		
9	40	3/2/38/0/20	4/2/38/0/20
10	60	3/3/57/0/30	4/3/57/0/30
11	38	3/2/38/0/19	4/2/38/0/19
12	58	3/3/57/0/29	4/3/57/0/29
13	29	3/3/57/0/29	
14	0		
15	29	4/3/57/0/29	
16	0		
17	0		

Note: The TOTAL SOLD column will be printed if the firm purchases that particular market research study. It will give the total seats sold in each market by all firms in that market. The sales figures shown above for markets 1 to 5 are the same as the five markets each firm is operating in. Refer to Table 8 for the current market numbers that your company (number) has been assigned.

The Seats offered per day is calculated by multiplying the number of flights flown per day times the seats (capacity) of the type aircraft used in that market. Example in Market 1: 2 flights × 19 seats per aircraft = 38

CRITICAL NOTE REGARDING SEATS AND FLIGHTS OFFERED

If you enter more flights than your aircraft can fly in a day (greater than 1,800 miles per day), the maintenance program will be shortchanged and the aircraft could/will suffer serious mechanical problems. In addition, the FAA will issue a substantial fine to your firm for lack of required maintenance. All of the costs of flying the aircraft will increase as well (maintenance, flight operations, fuel, and overtime for passenger service personnel). *It does not pay to enter incorrect values on the decision form!*

NOTES ON THE QUARTERLY REPORT

Revenues on the Income Statement

Your revenues are calculated by the passenger miles flown multiplied by the average fare on a passenger-mile basis.

Marketing Expenses

Your marketing expenses include both advertising and promotion budgets as well as the salaries for outside salespersons at $12,000 per quarter. All three of these items will be included in the total for "Marketing Expenses" on the income and expense statement.

Additional Employee Compensation

The report provides the employee turnover percentage, actual number of employees leaving during the quarter, and the additional cost of this turnover, which is listed on the income statement as "Hiring/OJT Cost."

If you refer to the Quarter 0 report, you will notice that the firm had a turnover of 7 employees in quarter 0 and the cost of this is listed under Hiring/OJT costs, i.e., $7 \times \$3,000 = \$21,000$.

Interest Expense

Interest expense is the cost of your short-term and long-term loans. Interest is calculated on the loan balances as shown on the current Balance Sheet. If an overdraft loan is needed, this interest cost will appear the quarter AFTER the loan is required. The reason for this is that the loan was granted on the last day of the quarter and was due to be paid off in the following quarter along with the interest due. However, as with all short-term loans, you must specify a loan payment by inserting the amount preceded by a minus sign.

Interest Income on Certificates of Deposit

The interest on your Certificates of Deposit will be shown. The rate of interest is 5% per year.

Lease Payments

Lease payments represent the amount due for all aircraft that are leased. Since these are operating leases, the aircraft do not appear on the balance sheet as an asset. Leases will be granted for an indefinite period, but there is a $50,000 fee to cancel the lease and return the aircraft to the lessor. The firm does not have any aircraft under lease at the current time.

Other Profits/Losses

If other sources of income become available during the simulation, the net income after expenses will be shown under the category "Other Profits or Losses" on the income statement. If you have more than one additional source of income in a quarter, both will be totaled in this figure.

Accounts Receivable

Only 60% of the gross revenues each quarter appear as a cash source because that is all that was collected by the end of the quarter. You may expect the 40% balance to be a cash income next quarter; this balance is shown on the Balance Sheet as Accounts Receivable. There is no method of increasing or decreasing the 60% – 40% schedule.

Accounts Payable

Only 70% of the expenses had been paid by the end of the quarter and the balance of 30% is shown as Accounts Payable on the Balance Sheet. In addition, expenses due to travel agency commissions (10%) plus customer refunds (as determined by your reliability factor) will be paid during the current quarter. Note: The entry "70% of operating expenses" on the Cash Flow statement is 70% of operating expenses LESS depreciation, since depreciation is *not* a cash expense.

Overdraft Loan

If the total cash available is not sufficient to meet cash demands, your bank will automatically issue your firm an overdraft loan. This loan will cover your cash shortage exactly and your Ending Cash will show a zero balance. The interest for this loan is not charged until the following quarter.

Retained Earnings

Retained Earnings is an accounting entry of all past profits less dividends paid. It represents the profits that have not been paid out to stockholders but have been retained by the firm for growth needs. Retained earnings have been used for various assets and do not represent cash!

Other Data on the Report

The productivity section of your report shows TOTAL REVENUE PASSENGERS boarded for the quarter. Your airline operates 80 days per quarter, which includes 5 weekdays and more limited service on weekends. The TOTAL MILES FLOWN per quarter is a reflection of all your trips in all your markets. The MAXIMUM MILEAGE your fleet may safely and efficiently fly is listed in this section.

✔ If you fly over your maximum mileage, your costs will escalate and you will be fined by the FAA.

AVAILABLE SEAT MILES is the number of seats available on all of your routes and can be calculated by multiplying the seats available per flight by the miles in the particular market. Then add all these individual markets for the total.

REVENUE PASSENGER MILES (RPM) is that portion of available seat miles that actually had a paying passenger. This is calculated by multiplying the total passengers flown on each flight by the length of the flight in miles by the total flights each quarter. (This is a difficult calculation but it is done easily by the computer program!)

Your *PASSENGER LOAD FACTOR* is a ratio of revenue passenger miles divided by available seat miles. This indicates the average percentage of seats occupied. You will need from 50% to 56% to breakeven. The *YIELD PER REVENUE PASSENGER MILE* is obtained by dividing revenues by revenue passenger miles.

The *COST PER AVAILABLE SEAT MILE* is calculated by dividing total operating costs (including commissions and refunds) by seat miles. This will indicate how much it is costing to fly one seat one mile (whether occupied or not). The *YIELD PER AVAILABLE SEAT MILE* is total revenues divided by available seat miles; this indicates the revenue for each seat flown one mile.

CALCULATING BREAKEVEN LOAD: An easy method of determining your breakeven load is to divide the cost per Available Seat Mile by the Yield per Revenue Passenger Mile. To use quarter 0 as an example: .178/.35 = .509. Therefore a 50.9% passenger load is the airline's Breakeven Point.

EMPLOYEE TURNOVER information is given along with total employees at the end of the quarter and employees lost due to turnover during the quarter. To decrease employee turnover, the firm must pay higher wages and increase the training budget.

32

The *SHORT-TERM INTEREST RATE* for each firm can also be different, according to the overall financial condition of the firm. At this point, the firm is being charged 2% over the current prime rate for short-term loans (10%) and 9% for long-term loans. The firm's interest rates as well as the prime rate could change during the course of the simulation.

The *LINE OF CREDIT* for each firm is different and is a function of the bank's credit practices at the time a loan is negotiated and the firm's financial health and financial history. *Normally*, the line of credit is equal to four times the total equity of the firm less total liabilities. If the decision entry program will not allow you to enter this estimated value, you will be notified of this when you attempt to enter a loan amount in the decision entry program.

FUEL PRICES are quoted for the open market in the current quarter (spot prices) and for the three-month contract for next quarter. There is no forecast for spot fuel prices as they are determined on a day-to-day basis during the quarter.

Stock Price and Shares Outstanding

The price of stock is based on several factors: book value (total equity divided by shares outstanding), earnings per share, dividends paid, return on sales, earnings trend, and other factors more subjective in nature, such as good cash management, reasonable flight reliability, financial stability, and profit consistency. The number of outstanding SHARES OF COMMON STOCK is also given. The stock price in the industry can be very volatile from quarter to quarter, so do not be discouraged by temporary setbacks!

✔ Do not make your decisions with the single goal of increasing your stock price. You will be *chasing* the stock price the entire duration of the simulation and not applying your strategy in operating the firm. If you stay focused on your operating strategy, profits should/will follow.

News Messages and Other Occurrences

Some occurrences have a cause-and-effect relationship, and your team will be able to respond with corrective action. *Other occurrences are strictly accidents of fate in operating an airline.* Some messages on the team's report are factual, while others are industry rumors. You need to discuss the importance of the messages to your team and discern which is which!

Mergers (if approved by your instructor)

Anytime after quarter 5 you may merge with another firm in your industry (e.g., class), *if* your instructor allows mergers. The merger will be a "paper" merger as there is no method of combining balance sheets within the computer program. In essence, a holding company is formed and the two airlines operate as separate profit centers for the remainder of the simulation. One of the advantages is that you can share market research information and save expenses. You can also rearrange your route structure so you are not competing in any markets; this relieves some of your equivalent to boost other markets. In addition, a sharing of successful strategy during the succeeding quarters may help each team become more efficient and effective.

You will need to change the names of both airlines to reflect the merger; an example: TransAir East and TransAir West. To reflect this change in the computer, place the company number of the firm you've merged with as the right-hand two digits of your quality budget each quarter (e.g., $20,011 indicates this firm has merged with company 11). In addition, inform your instructor in writing of this merger. One of the benefits of merging is that the business of one airline will help boost traffic in the other because it is assumed that you share one or more hubs.

There are certain decisions that need to be common with both firms. These are fare and cabin service. Other decisions that should be common but not required are (1) employee compensation, (2) maintenance level, and 3) incident response. For purposes of any common class activities, such as a stockholders' meeting or final audit report, consult with your instructor as to whether these should be done by the entire merged group or by each team independently.

✔ **Each team in the merger must place the notation in the quality budget as indicated above.**

TABLE 11
OPERATING HISTORY PRECEDING 8 QUARTERS

Period	Revenue Passen-ger Miles	Available seat miles	Cost per Revenue Passenger Mile	Yield per Available Seat Mile	Load Factor	Net Profits	Fuel - Spot/ Contract
Startup	4,259,321	8,147,200	.178	.183	52.2%	$24,116	.96/.96
Q-1	3,976,427	8,147,200	.152	.183	48.8%	$8,450	1.01/.93
Q-2	3,492,145	7,463,400	.149	.182	46.7%	$3,520	.99/.94
Q-3	2,897,566	7,463,400	.141	.180	38.8%	−$205	.98/.96
Q-4	2,680,345	7,463,400	.140	.180	35.9%	−$5,872	.94/1.01
Q-5	2,344,965	5,320,650	.147	.183	44.0%	$2,156	.92/1.00
Q-6	2,202,798	5,320,650	.139	.181	41.4%	$435	.93/1.00
Q-7	1,983,388	5,320,650	.135	.181	37.2%	−$6,310	.95/.96

The airline you are taking over has been in business a few years but lacks much meaningful historical data due to its size and limited record-keeping. It began with 9 seat aircraft and slowly traded up plane by plane until it achieved its present fleet 2 years ago. That is the period of time shown on the table above. You will note the fluctuation of fuel prices. Since fuel is a large expenditure for an airline, your management team should follow the trends carefully and contract for fuel when it is prudent to do so.

TABLE 10
U. S. REGIONAL AND MAJOR AIRLINE HUBS

ANCHORAGE	Alaska Airlines
ATLANTA	Delta
BALTIMORE	U. S. Air, Southwest
CHARLOTTE	U. S. Air
CHICAGO	American, United
CINCINNATI	Delta
CLEVELAND	Continental
COLUMBUS	America West
DALLAS/FORT WORTH	American, Delta
DENVER	United
DETROIT	Northwest
FORT WORTH	Southwest
HOUSTON	Continental
INDIANAPOLIS	U. S. Air
LAS VEGAS	America West
LOS ANGELES	Delta
MEMPHIS	Northwest
MIAMI	American
MINNEAPOLIS/ST PAUL	Northwest
NEWARK	Continental
NEW YORK	TWA (Merged with American)
ORLANDO	Delta
PHILADELPHIA	U. S. Air
PHOENIX	America West
PITTSBURGH	U. S. Air
PORTLAND	Alaska Airlines
ST. LOUIS	TWA (Merged with American)
SALT LAKE CITY	Delta
SAN FRANCISCO	United
SEATTLE	Alaska Airlines
WASHINGTON, D.C.	United

This chart is for general information only and does not pertain to the markets in the simulation. Your team may use this to better understand how the hub-and-spoke system works. You may want to assume a hub city from above and choose spoke cities approximating the distances involved to add realism to the simulation. Due to the rapid changes in the airline industry, the chart above may have changed since the printing of the manual.

This section contains 15 *incidents*, enough for each decision period. The incidents are identified A through O with two additional optional exercises. Use Incident A for quarter 1. Thereafter, the incident to be used will be printed on your firm's quarterly report. Make a decision concerning each incident and enter your response on the decision form. Your instructor may want you to write the rationale for your decision and submit it (only one form to be turned in for each team). The two optional incidents have no consequences but are more of an "Optional Assignment" that may be assigned by your instructor. The incidents follow:

A	Naming Your Airline
B	Press Release or Not?
C	Channels of Distribution
D	Competitor's Safety Problem
E	Diversification–Auto Rental
F	Dual Designate
G	The Charter Trip
H	Hire Competitor's Employees
I	Hiring Decision
J	Purchasing Policies
K	Advertising Campaign
L	Air Ambulance Service
M	Flight for Congressman
N	Kickback Problem
O	Diversification Planning

Optional Exercise 1: Passenger Bill of Rights
Optional Exercise 2: List of Employee Policies

Incident A: Naming Your Airline   Industry ____ Quarter____ Company ____

This form should be submitted to the instructor with the decisions for the first quarter.

One of the most important decisions a new firm makes is naming the business. Often the first contact prospective customers have is when they phone the airline to make a reservation. When the operator answers, doesn't *Americana Airlines* sound more professional than *DJS Air?* In fact, your instructor *may* build in demand for your airline after ranking the names of all the firms in the industry.

Although you can rename your airline if the first name selected turns out unsatisfactory or the strategy of your airline changes, it is important to select a name that would stand the test of time and perhaps even be adaptable to a new strategy if you desired to change your strategy sometime during the simulation play. However, it may be strategically sound to change the name of your business if it (1) gains publicity; (2) helps get rid of an old image; and/or (3) expresses the NEW image. For example, if you decide to affiliate with a large carrier (e.g., American), you may want to change your name to take advantage of the connection, AMERICAN EAGLE. If you later decide to become a luxury or low-price carrier, you may want to express your new strategy in a new name, e.g., Translux or Western Econlines.

Some factors you may want to take into consideration in naming your business and some right/wrong examples are:

1.   Is the name descriptive of what you do?
     Pony Express vs. Trans-American Airlines

2.   Is the name descriptive of your service?
     Luxury Airline vs. Northeast Lines

3.   Is the name an ego trip or does it contain meaningless names/words representing the owners?
     DWT Airlines (first initials of the owners) or We Three Airlines

4.   Is the name distinctive, perhaps catchy, and easy to remember? Will it be conducive to future advertising jingles and logos? Eastern Econo Airlines vs. JanSanMark Airlines

5.   Does the name lend itself to future changes in services or expansion of the product line (example: cargo, charters)?   Pete's Passenger Express vs. Americana Airlines

Of course, some of the factors above have conflicting requirements. You will need to determine which factors are most important for your team's needs. The worksheet on the reverse side may aid in selecting a name.

Enter a zero on the decision form for Incident A.

LIST YOUR SERVICE (major purpose or mission):

_____

_____

LIST OTHER SERVICES YOU THINK YOU MIGHT WANT TO ADD IN THE FUTURE, IF ANY (Example: You will be given the opportunity to begin cargo service and auto rental in the simulation):

_____

_____

DESCRIBE YOUR "TARGET MARKET" (the demographics of the segment of the population you want to serve. Example: *"Scot Air, the low price leader.")*

_____

_____

_____

LIST SOME ADVERTISING MOTTOS, JINGLES, OR LINES YOU THINK YOUR TARGET MARKET MIGHT RELATE TO (Example: *"Fly Sublime the On-time Airline."):*

_____

_____

_____

DESCRIBE THE MOTIF (cabin design, color schemes, aircraft paint design) you may use. (Example: A recent airline chose the color *blue* and chose the name "Jet Blue."

_____

_____

_____

_____

DESCRIBE ANY OTHER FACTORS THAT YOU WANT TO CONSIDER IN NAMING YOUR BUSINESS:

_____

_____

_____

FROM THE DATA ABOVE, WRITE AT LEAST FOUR POSSIBLE NAMES:

1. _____
2. _____
3. _____
4. _____

SELECT THE BEST NAME: _____

DESCRIBE THE OVERRIDING REASON FOR ITS SELECTION:

_____

_____

_____

INCIDENT B: Press Release or Not?

The station manager at one of the cities you serve just called and reported that the captain of the aircraft that just landed had keeled over in the cockpit as the plane was about to land. The first officer quickly took the controls, circled the field as he pushed the captain's limp body away from the controls and safely landed the aircraft. The aircraft was met by an ambulance and the captain was taken to the hospital for observation. Except for surprise at the turn of events, the passengers did not know of the potentially dangerous situation that had occurred. The station manager made this call to headquarters before the press came around for a statement. He believed that the passengers had all left the terminal without talking to anyone from the press but could not be sure. He was asking your headquarters staff for advice.

A staff meeting was quickly called. One of the officials felt that, since the passengers were not fully aware of the situation, the whole affair should be kept as quiet as possible. Another said that sooner or later the press would find out and demand a response. In addition, a report would have to be made to the FAA within 24 hours. Once that report was made, the records would become available to the press under the open records law. Another staff member thought the affair should be kept quiet until pressure was put on the airline for information. "Perhaps the whole thing will dissipate on its own, within time," he said. Another believed that honesty was the best policy although it could radically hurt business; the flying public may be turned off by the incident and refuse to fly the airline until some time had passed. A lively debate followed but the phone soon rang and a report from the hospital said the captain had had a mild heart attack but would be OK. This was even worse news than if it had merely been an episode of heartburn. Here are the choices available:

1. Quickly prepare a press release saying the captain had suffered some type of mishap and had to be taken to the hospital. No other details would be released. As one staff member put it, "Give them something but not the whole story. This could be very harmful to our image."

2. Advise all members of the company to adhere to a *no comment* policy and hope the whole thing will be quickly forgotten."After all," stated one person, "we are under no obligation to tell the pubic everything that happens around here."

3. Prepare a succinct press release, as described below, along with a "no further comment" notice to the staff: "The captain aboard flight 27 became ill during the flight and was taken to the hospital upon landing for observation."

4. Send the CEO on a quick "business trip" and respond to all inquires with "The CEO is not available and company policy states that only he/she can make announcements about the airline." It is hoped this action will take the immediate heat off the situation and it will be forgotten by most people by the time the CEO returns a week later.

5. Prepare a press release that gives <u>all</u> the details of the incident. It should be noted that this action could have serious public relations repercussions.

6. One staff member believes the airline can gain positive publicity by releasing the following press release: "First Officer Larry Jonesz took heroic action in saving the aircraft and passengers in a potentially serious situation through his fast action in the cockpit, ...etc."

Select the one that you feel is the closest to the action you should take and place it on your decision form.

INCIDENT C: Channels of Distribution-Dot Com?

Historically, about 90% of the tickets sold by airlines have been processed through travel agents who are awarded a commission of about 10% of the ticket price. In the past two decades, these transactions have been conducted through computer reservation systems owned by the airlines themselves. Recently, the channel of sales has migrated to the Internet through the use of both independently-owned and airline-owned online travel services. In order for this to work, however, the airlines have had to upload their constantly changing fare structures as well as paying a commission on each ticket sold. Today, most airlines also sell their tickets online directly from their own Web site at slightly reduced prices. If they issue an electronic ticket to the customer (no actual paper ticket is issued), there is even a lower cost of ticketing, since the transaction is consummated through computer links at the airport without additional paper trails.

As the simulation opens, your company is still selling directly to the customer through phone banks or issuing tickets through travel agents and corporate travel accounts. You recognize that new customers are less likely to buy tickets through these channels. In considering your strategy, you must take into account the fact that one of your largest travel agents has threatened to give the tickets on your routes to your competitor(s). You may change your mechanism for ticket sales as follows:

1. Maintain your phone banks and travel agent relationships. Offer electronic tickets at a 4% discount. This will also decrease your cost of operations slightly.

2. Join several Web consortiums for ticket sales. Maintain your telephone access. Commissions to the consortiums are 3% of sales along with the possibility that you will generate some new demand. The consortium, which has the advantage of having several independent sites, would charge 5% to you in commission and give the customer a 2 to 5% discount.

3. Maintain your telephone bank and open a Web site of your own for ticket sales. You will have a one time $20,000 startup cost but no commissions will need to be paid on tickets sold on the Web. Discount the tickets 2 to 5% to the customers that order through your web site.

4. In order to avoid the additional expense of managing a Web site, contract with owners of a large, nationally-known site to sell tickets. Their ability to get you on their Web site within two weeks has great appeal. Sales should increase with such a well-known site. They would charge you 5% for each ticket sold and would also sell the tickets at a 2 to 5% discount. No front-end cost.

Enter your decision (1, 2, 3, or 4) on your decision form.

Note: The results of this incident is in addition to the small number of sales currently generated by your advertising budget that is triggered by placing a "2" in the budget signally web sales. (See page 4).

INCIDENT D: Competitor's Safety Problem

Your maintenance chief has reported that a mechanic you hired from another regional airline told him that the other airline did a lot of "pencil maintenance." That is, they wrote a lot of things in the maintenance logs that did not actually get done – required inspections, repairs, and parts replacements. He said "The outfit is just a big accident, waiting to happen." Your maintenance chief wanted to report it to the executive committee to see what, if anything, should be done. He stated that the mechanic reported that he quit that airline because he did not like to be associated with such an activity. The other airline has competed against you in the past and is likely to compete in at least one market in the future. It has a reputation of being very aggressive competitively.

Which of the following actions should you take?

1.   Report the incident to the FAA (the other airline will be able to ascertain who made the report).

2.   Phone the president of the other airline and tell him what you heard . You are on neutral terms with that person as he is your competitor.

3.   Drop a tip to the local investigative reporter at the newspaper.

4.   Report it to an official of the Airline Association. You cannot be sure that the official or the association will take any action, but at least your conscience will be clear. It is somewhat possible that your name may be leaked to the competitor if you make this report.

5.   You determine that the matter is either (1) none of your business or (2) that the report is just "sour grapes" from a disgruntled employee. So you decide to do nothing.

Enter your decision (1, 2, 3, 4, or 5) on the decision form.

INCIDENT E: Diversification – Auto Rental

During the last meeting of your management team, the planning officer presented a proposal for diversifying. It was to acquire a rental car agency at the smallest city you are currently serving. While there is a car rental agency located downtown at a service station and a locally owned taxi service serves the airport, there is no car rental agency serving the airport. Although the total passengers boarded daily there is modest, quite a few people do inquire about the availability of rental cars. Your local station manager is very excited about the prospects of building up a reasonable rental business there and wants the opportunity to try it.

A firm that has been very successful at franchising such operations is interested in supporting your efforts. This firm would sublease autos to you as needed and provide insurance coverage (insurance is difficult to obtain for small operations such as this). The firm would guarantee the availability of enough autos to handle 90% of the business 90% of the time; in other words, it is not profitable to keep an expensive inventory for the few times of high demand.

The start-up costs would be $200,000. This would pay for the cost of the initial franchise fee, advertising, paving of a small storage lot, and rebuilding your ticket counter to include space for the retail business. Although the start-up costs are higher than the package business, the payoff possibilities are also higher. Again, extensive cost and revenue studies have been made. They indicate a high probability of success but conflicting data on HOW successful.

Starting losses of from $3,000 to $10,000 per quarter could be expected the first one or two quarters. After that, there is a 10% probability of just breaking even, a 60% probability of making $60,000 per quarter, and 30% probability of making between $60,000 and $100,000 per quarter.

The director of marketing focused on the crux of the matter as she noted, "After making a cost-benefit analysis of both propositions, it will boil down to the question, 'What business are we in–or, what businesses should we be in?' It is an important strategic question. Personally, I think we should be in the TRANSPORTATION business and this acquisition would fit that mission."

The financial vice president responded with a worried look, "Yes, but it will take financial resources away from our passenger airline business. Are we strong enough to take on something new?"

Another staff member responded, "A competitor may chose to pick up the franchise if we don't. Perhaps we should consider it as a defensive strategy and not necessarily one in which we plan to make a profit."

The president added, "Does this *fit* with our strategic plans?"

Due to simulation constraints, this is not an option later in the game. Place the number of your response on your decision form and explain your rationale on this sheet, including the mathematical calculation you may have used to aid in making the decision. Turn this sheet in to your instructor. Note: Costs of starting this business will be allocated over eight quarters.

1. Begin the auto rental business.
2. Do not begin the auto rental business.

Select one of the choices above and place it on your decision form.

INCIDENT F: Dual Designate

Your airline has been offered the opportunity to dual-designate with a major carrier at your regional hub. This carrier is a profitable major company with a history of good passenger service and safety. Dual designation allows all of your markets to be listed with the listing of the larger carrier in the computer reservation system and in its published schedules. You thus become the *spoke operation* for smaller communities. Although some autonomy is sacrificed by the feeder carrier, sales will increase.

Currently, you routinely hold your outgoing runs from your hub until the major carriers have brought passengers into the hub. However, they do not delay their departures for your connecting passengers. The major carrier with which you are discussing dual designation has stated it will work closely with you on both departure and incoming flights. Examples of these types of agreements in the industry are numerous. They include U. S. Air Express, Delta Connection, American Eagle, Continental Express, and Northwest Airlink.

The vice president of marketing feels the move would be an "excellent opportunity" and one that would "assure the future of the airline." The president knows some of the stockholders would prefer not to give up the image, name, and autonomous operation of the firm. The director of planning has expressed concern about the contractual ability of the major carrier to control scheduling and route structure. The VP of finance countered this objection with "I don't think there's a future for independent airlines without some type of connection with a major carrier. If we pass this up we may not get the same opportunity again with a carrier of this stature. I think we should accept or we will slowly be squeezed out by other carriers who have taken advantage of aligning with a major carrier."

The carrier with whom you are negotiating asks that you repaint your fleet with its colors and insignias at a cost of $30,000 per aircraft. (This cost will be allocated over the next ten periods.) Your airline will also be renamed to indicate your connection with the carrier. Your schedules will be dictated by the schedule of the major carrier. There may be some change in your routes.

The options are:

1. Accept the offer. The successful firm(s) will be notified next quarter and any costs will be charged automatically at that time.

2. Make a counteroffer to become an informal "feeder" for the major carrier's operation but retain your name and right to schedule routes. (If another firm agrees to accept the offer [option 1], it is unlikely the major airline would accept this counteroffer.)

3. Investigate the possibility of merging with another commuter airline to provide the financial and fleet strength to become a strong independent regional airline. (See page 34.)

4. Continue as an independent operation using computer-aided scheduling techniques to optimize your ability to connect with major carrier flights.

Place your decision (1, 2, 3, or 4) on the decision form. You will be informed on the next quarterly report if the negotiations were successful.

INCIDENT G: The Charter Trip

On Friday afternoon you received a call from a gentleman who identified himself as the CEO (Chief Executive Officer) of a firm in a small city about 100 miles from your headquarters. He wanted to charter an aircraft to make a trip to a small U.S. border town. He assured you that you would not be required to fly over the border into a foreign country or deal with customs agents. The trip would depart tomorrow (Saturday) evening, make a two-hour stop at the town's airport, and return sometime after midnight Sunday morning.

The caller cautioned you about the confidentiality of the trip and requested that your two "most closed-mouthed" pilots fly the charter. In reply to some serious and repeated questions concerning the mission and legality of the trip and/or cargo, the caller assured you that the trip was for legal business purposes and no contraband would be involved. He alluded to "a highly sensitive business matter" that would have an enormous effect on his firm if "the parties can agree."

The aircraft you would have available to send is in good condition and its maintenance schedule is up-to-date; thus the trip would not endanger the readiness of the aircraft for its normal schedule the following Sunday.

The prospective customer has offered you a fee that would net your firm $5,000 profit above the direct costs. The fee is somewhat large, considering the length of the trip, but the caller offered it and you did not object.

A check of the telephone directory of the caller's city did indicate a telephone number and street address for the firm. Due to the lateness in the day and the fact that the next day is Saturday, you could not obtain any further information about the firm.

Your director of marketing is urging you to take the charter due to the potential profit and future business this firm might provide. "I've heard of the company. They're in air conditioning or something like that. I've also heard they're either trying to acquire another company or they're about to be acquired. This might be the final closing of the deal."

1. Take the charter trip.
2. Do not take the charter trip.

Place your decision (1 or 2) on your decision form.

46

INCIDENT H: Hire Competitor's Employees

Due to the expansion possibilities brought about by the effects of deregulation and a good demand forecast, you are considering adding a salesperson to your staff. A competing airline, which is larger than yours, has a sales manager who has built a large corporate customer base. Because of her pleasant personality and convincing style, she has been able to successfully cultivate the travel agents in the region as well as sign several corporations for steady charter business. One of your friends believes she can be lured away from her current employer with a bonus of $10,000.

Another important position for your firm to consider is that of director of maintenance. This area can either make or break an airline in a hurry. Complete and timely record keeping is a requirement of the FAA and one that gets many airlines in trouble. Parts inventory management as well as mechanic and aircraft maintenance scheduling are also crucial elements to an effective and efficient maintenance operation. A talented director is working for another competitor of yours, and he could probably be lured away for a bonus of $10,000.

Two of your owners discuss the situation: "I just don't like taking an employee from a competitor. It's bad business--they could turn around and hire one of the people we've invested a lot in. Don't we have a responsibility to competitors as well as to our passengers and staff?"

"I don't think so; after all, business is business! Besides, the employees are making the free choice to move-we're just offering them the kind of salary their current employer should have offered them!"

Enter your response (1, 2, 3, or 4) on the decision form.

1. Hire the salesperson. Other expense will be charged $10,000. (Also, hire one salesperson on line 5 of the decision form.)

2. Hire the director of maintenance. Other expense will be charged $10,000 for the bonus.

3. Hire both. Other expense will be charged $20,000. (To implement this, hire one salesperson on line 5 of the decision form.) The expense includes the bonus for #2 and hiring expenses for #1.

4. Hire neither.

Note: If you want to hire a salesperson this quarter but not the person described above, you may do so by entering that hire on the decision form as usual.

INCIDENT I: Hiring Decision

There will be a vacancy for a station manager soon. The station manager is the top manager in one of the airline's airports and is responsible for all activities at the airport, from ticketing passengers to handling the fueling and turnaround of an aircraft. The station manager usually supervises one or two ticket clerks, two baggage handlers, and one or more aircraft servicing people. He/she works from the first flight in the morning until the last flight at night, often a 12-hour day, five-to-six days a week. He/she must be good with the public and very passenger oriented – when anything out of the ordinary happens, it falls on the station manager to make things right with the passengers. The station with the opening currently has an all white, male crew. The only requirement in the job advertisement is that the applicant have "related experience in the airline industry." You have pared the list of applicants down to the following four individuals:

1. A middle-aged minority female who was formerly a cabin attendant for an airline that went bankrupt. She received excellent annual evaluations and one award for "Cabin Attendant of the Year." She is bright, articulate, and seems to be highly motivated. She stated that she can learn technical parts of the job quickly (supervision of baggage handling, fueling, restocking the aircraft, etc.). She is the only applicant with a four-year college degree. One of your staff people stated, "If we are going to stay ahead of the EEOC on affirmative action, now is the time to start."

2. A middle-aged white male who was assistant station manager for five years for a large airline who wanted to relocate. He appears to be pleasant and easy-going and has good recommendations from his former employer. He could step in and immediately do the job well.

3. The ticket agent at the airport where the opening has occurred has applied. She has been working for the airline two years and has had very good performance evaluations. She worked as a baggage handler a few times when needed but has not done some of the other jobs she would be supervising. The outgoing station manager has stated, "I think, in time, she could learn how to be a good station manager. She may make some mistakes but everybody does. The company should send a strong message to employees that promotion from within is our policy. In addition, Southwest Airlines believes *hire for attitude and train for job knowledge*. I think we should follow that policy."

4. The son of the owner of the largest employer in town has just graduated with a two-year associate degree from a well-known aviation management program. He is very mature for his age (28) and a sharp individual. He did have academic training in station management in his aviation program. The bonus in hiring this young person is that the airline would undoubtedly get all the business from his father's firm, which *is substantial*, since he brings people in from all over the U.S. to his plant. His father is very influential in the city and has made it known to the president of your airline that he would consider it a personal favor if the airline hired his son.

Place your response (1, 2, 3, or 4) on your decision form.

INCIDENT J: Purchasing Policies

During the last meeting of your management team, the chief financial officer presented a plan to phase out the airline's major supplier of expendable supplies (such as oil, tires, hydraulic fluids, and other parts). He had received a bid from a competing firm (Apex) to provide these supplies at an annual savings of at least $10,000. The director of maintenance spoke against the proposal:

"I know that Apex Suppliers are a little less expensive but our current supplier, Vest Brothers, has been a very dependable supplier; they've shipped items needed in an emergency on Saturdays, Sundays, and holidays. They've always taken back any overstock item and given full credit to us. Although Apex Suppliers have a decent reputation, I don't think they'll give us the same service we're currently getting. It takes a long time to learn to work together like we do with Vest; price isn't everything!"

The vice-president of finance responded, "Well, Apex has assured me they will give even BETTER service and provide electronic data interchange (EDI) for ordering and billing; this will reduce lost or misplaced supplies and parts by 10%. If they don't perform as promised, we have a 30-day cancellation clause built into the contract. Remember, we've given Vest Brothers a chance to bid again and they've told us they're at rock bottom prices now. But I personally think that if we continued to play one against the other we could get even lower prices."

The worried maintenance chief retorted, "I like the idea of savings of 10%. But if it doesn't work out with Apex and we want to get Vest back, we'll have to start building the relationship again. And anyway, don't we have some responsibility to suppliers as well as our other publics?"

"Not if the suppliers can't meet the competition's prices," retorted the VP.

What should your firm do?

Place the number of your response on your decision form.

1. Exemplary service pays: keep your current supplier (Vest).

2. Business is business; the bottom line is all-important. Switch to the lower bidder (Apex).

3. Attempt to continue to work with both suppliers, working one against the other until an even better deal emerges.

INCIDENT K: Advertising Campaign

Your salesperson reported her concern over some grapevine information that she picked up during her last tour of travel agencies. A few of the agents are reporting that potential passengers seem to be booking reservations on competing airlines. The reasons given are:

a. Although you run promotional fares occasionally, passengers report that the restrictions are so tight and the available seats set aside for these fares are so limited that they cannot buy tickets at the advertised fees.

b. Your advertisements claim you are the *On-time airline – The airline with the best on-time record.* However, your record is not much better or worse than that of your competitors but you have been advertising this slogan so long that many of the (infrequent) traveling public believe it! Frequent travelers on your airline know of your somewhat average record and joke about the ad.

Some facts:

You are aware that airline passengers are not "brand loyal." Therefore, advertising is a way of putting your name in front of the public. Most people are leery of advertising anyway, so you feel you must compete with other airlines in any way you can, as long as it is legal. Statistics from the Regional Airline Association indicate that a significant portion of passengers who request a promotional fare will buy a ticket at the regular fare if there are no discount seats available.

While you are aware of the average reliability record of your airline, your marketing manager insists that "harmless trade puffery" is standard business practice and, until someone brings suit against the firm, it should continue using this very successful slogan.

Here are several options:

1. Run a promotional campaign to explain your promotional fare rules and why ALL seats cannot be sold at these low fares. This should improve your credibility with the travel agents and the public somewhat. The cost is $10,000.

2. Cease using "The on-time airline" as a slogan and replace it with something more catchy, clever, cute, or honest, or all four! The ad agency fee is $5,000.

3. Option one and two. Combined cost is $12,000.

4. Do nothing. These are normal business problems and tactics.

Place your response (1, 2, 3, or 4) on your decision form. Any costs will be charged automatically to other expenses.

Note to teams: While your team may feel that this type of thing would never be approved in the first place, assume that it did happen. Actually, it did occur to the airline on which this simulation was modeled.

INCIDENT L: Air Ambulance Service

Your firm has been approached by a large hospital in one of the cities you are currently serving to provide air transportation for certain critically ill patients. These patients would need to be brought in to the hospital from various cities in your geographical area and, in some cases, flown back to their hometown or the hospital at their home city for further recuperation. The prospective client has built a reputation for performing a particularly complicated medical procedure and is one of the few hospitals in the country that can perform this procedure. The trips would be made on an "as needed" basis and would be taken after regular scheduled hours (i.e., from 10 p.m. until 6 a..m.). Each charter would bring in revenues averaging $3,000.

To take on this business opportunity, you need to equip one aircraft with medical equipment and stretcher tie-downs. This would cost $12,000.

The accounting for this special charter business would be kept separately and any profits or losses would be shown under OTHER PROFITS/LOSSES on the Income Statement. It is assumed that your smallest aircraft would be used for this service. Revenue and cost estimates indicate the gross profits could be as little as a few thousand dollars to as much as $20,000 per quarter.

Your president states, "I think it would be a great public relations move to take this project on. We have aircraft sitting on the ground at several cities overnight, positioned for the early morning run and this project could be done without repositioning any aircraft."

The director of maintenance responds, "Our routes are spread out far enough now without going to a lot of cities where we don't have maintenance facilities. I don't think we should do it. Besides, we're in the passenger business, not the charter business."

The vice-president of finance interjects, "I do not agree with you. We're in the transportation business and this is transportation! In addition, I've looked at the cost/income projections with the hospital staff and I think it will pay off. Even if we just break even, it's a great public image move. We have a few pilots who have even agreed to fly for free if it is a charity case."

Due to simulation constraints, this is not an option later in the game. Place the number of your response on your decision form, explain your rationale on this sheet and turn it in to your instructor. If you do not own one of the aircraft listed below, you must pass on this incident, as the other aircraft are too large and expensive to operate for this type of service.

1. Begin the service with the smallest aircraft in your fleet, a type A, B, C , D, or E aircraft.

2. Turn the offer down.

Place your response (1 or 2) on your decision form. Any costs will be charged automatically to other expenses.

INCIDENT M: Flight for Congressman

An official from the headquarters of your local Congressman called today. She is interested in having your airline provide shuttle service for the Congressman and/or his staff three to six times per month. The compensation would average $1,500 per flight; this amount covers the fuel and maintenance costs on your smallest aircraft. Trips would be scheduled a week in advance and the flights would not always occur on the same day of the week. Occasionally a Saturday trip might be requested.

Acceptance of the offer would give you access to this Congressman, who is on the Senate Military Transport Committee. This committee is responsible for final approval of contracts to private aviation companies who transport military personnel. You have some interest in this business, since it is potentially more steady than regularly scheduled passenger business and there are contracts available. One of the Congressman's aides hinted that a military contract would be the "reward" for offering your services. This could be a lucrative contract. In addition, the Congressman is also expected to be on the air transportation committee, if elected.

The irregularity in the Congressman's schedule might cause you some slight difficulty in operating your regularly scheduled routes. You figure that you can divert an aircraft from an unprofitable route if necessary; a Saturday run would require that you defer preventive maintenance on one aircraft for a week. What should you do?

Place your decision (1, 2, or 3) on your decision form.

1. Accept the offer. Your operations chief is clever and you believe that she/he will be able to solve any scheduling dilemmas.

2. Indicate that you are extremely interested; you can do business if they can provide a schedule at least two weeks in advance. (However, this action might result in the contract being awarded to a carrier that does not make this stipulation.)

3. Turn down the request.

INCIDENT N: Kickback Problem

An employee of one of your better travel agencies calls to inform you that your top salesman has been giving kickbacks to one or more employees of the agency. (If you don't have a salesman, it is one of your staff members who also makes sales calls.) In checking over his expense records, you find some irregularities on his expense account. The next morning you receive a call from one of your station managers who tells you he has confiscated an airline pass from the salesman's look-alike brother. The brother was trying to board a flight of yours and, when stopped, said his brother (your employee) had loaned him his pass. Your policy states that no one can use an employee's pass except the employee to whom it is issued. When you call the salesman (or staff member) in to discuss these problems, he denies kicking back any money and says that his brother must have picked up his pass when he was visiting last weekend. The salesman insists that he had no knowledge his brother had his pass.

Your management team has gathered to discuss what, if any, action to take against him. "Yes," stated the marketing manager, "he has been a naughty boy. But he is one of our top people and has brought in some nice contracts. He is a hard worker, and very loyal to the company. After all, we don't pay these people very much and if he wants to loan his pass to his brother, well, it is like a perk; employees can only fly if there is an empty seat so no real harm was done. And besides, I don't think we could have ever cracked that travel agency if he had not been good to their people. If he did make gifts of appreciation, they came out of his own pocket."

"What about the expense account irregularities?" asked the financial manager.

The marketing manager replied, "Well, if we paid our people better wages they wouldn't have to pad their expense accounts. Anyway, he was probably using it to tip the travel agent. He considered his generosity to the travel agent a simple *gratuity* for treating him and our company so nicely, and sending us business.

"After all, it is good business and a common business practice to give gifts of appreciation to good customers. Can we tell a guy how to use his own money?"

What should your firm do?

1. Tell him that you need the business from the travel agent and you don't want to know about any of his dealings. However, he should keep better track of his flight pass.

2. Have a talk with him and advise him that such practices must cease. Tell him that if word about this ever got to the other travel agents, the airline would be in a very embarrassing position.

3. Have a talk with him and tell him he is on probation for a year and that if anything else happens, he will be dismissed.

4. Dismiss him and replace him immediately. You need to send a message to all employees that the rules were made NOT to be broken. (If you do this, the program will automatically replace him with a new person. You do not need to do anything on the decision form under *Number of new salespersons hired.*)

Place your decision (1, 2, 3, or 4) on the decision form.

INCIDENT O: Diversification Planning

The planning officer of your airline has been gathering information concerning several opportunities for your firm. Since the climate seems good for additional common stock sales and bank loans, the possibilities of expansion through merger and acquisition seem very good. An opposite twist has also presented itself– an offer to purchase your airline! A thorough investigation and analysis by a competent financial analyst specializing in such matters will cost $3,000 for each item listed below and will be completed in three to nine months (with the exception of selection M which costs $3,001). This would be a necessary first step in pursuing any of these business opportunities.

Although these opportunities may not be possible before the end of the simulation, your instructor wants you to determine which you feel are appropriate. Indicate on a separate sheet of paper why your team chose each of the opportunities it did and turn it in to your instructor. Enter on the decision form the total amount you want to spend for the investigation(s), e.g., $6,000, 9,000,12,000, etc.

Risk factors as shown below are on a scale of very low risk (1) to very high risk (10). The risk factor takes into account the economic stability of that particular type of business, the difficulty in operating it, competition, and the profit potential.

A. Acquiring a food service company that serves several airlines. It is located in the airline's largest hub. The cost is $500,000 and the Return on Investment (ROI) is estimated to be in the 12% to 20% range with a risk factor of 5.

B. Going into the car rental business at one of your high-traffic cities. The facts are the same as presented in incident E except it is in a different city than depicted in that incident. Risk factor 5.

C. Begin a new company that would refurbish commuter aircraft. Due to the increasing cost of new aircraft, it is felt that many airlines would be interested in rebuilding and refurbishing their current fleet instead of purchasing a new fleet. The cost would be $2 million and the ROI is estimated to be in the 15% to 28% range with a risk factor of 6.

D. Acquiring a ground service business that serves eight cities, including three that you are currently serving. This type of business handles all baggage, refueling, interior cleaning and restocking of rest rooms, etc., for airlines. The parent company of the service wants to concentrate on businesses more in line with its other holdings and is willing to sell for $1 million. The ROI is estimated at 14% to 25% with a risk factor of 6.

E. Purchasing a small airline that is currently competing in two of your markets. The firm is operated efficiently and has seven Metroliners and one Jetstream; all aircraft and facilities are leased. The owner wishes to retire and is asking $2 million with liberal credit terms. ROI estimate is 20% to 30%; risk factor is 7.

F. Purchase a building for the firm's offices in a renovated downtown building with a prestigious address. A ten-year, 6% historical development loan is available. Cost $300,000. Savings in rent would be $30,000 per year.

G. Open a Fixed Base Operation (FBO) at one of your hub cities. An FBO fuels and maintains airline, business, and private aircraft; rents, leases, and sells aircraft. The facility could also serve as a minor repair station for your aircraft. The cost is $1 million and the ROI is 10% to 33%. The risk factor is 5.

-over-

INCIDENT O: Diversification Planning (continued)

H. Open a training facility for airline pilots. The center would specialize in offering the recurrent training required by the FAA to smaller airlines that cannot afford a facility of their own. A modern simulator would be acquired, which would be very enticing to many airlines. This diversification would allow your own pilots to train with the very latest technology. The cost would be $250,000; ROI of 15% to 20% and risk factor of 4.

I. Leasing three cargo jets, which you would operate exclusively for a large air-package service firm. The firm is willing to give a four-year contract with a clause that automatically adjusts the fees to reflect the current cost of fuel. The cost to establish the business (crew training, additional maintenance facilities and equipment) is $300,000. The ROI is 20% and the risk factor is 3 to 4.

J. Becoming the regional distributor for a new 19-passenger airliner built in Spain. It is a cabin class, pressurized, prop-jet aircraft with a restroom. The aircraft's strong features are its luxurious interior design and state-of-the-art cockpit. The manufacturer is willing to lease one of the aircraft to you to put in service and concurrently serve as a demonstrator for $72,000 per quarter. The aircraft sells for $4.2 million with a sales commission of 5%. The cost of establishing a sales office, critical parts inventory, and first-year marketing expenses is $250,000. The ROI could be negative or as high as 1000% if a large order is obtained. The risk factor is 7 to 8.

K. Refurbish waiting areas in all cities served with a new, upbeat motif, including new counters, signs, and furniture. Cost: $20,000 per city. This cost would be to conduct a market research study to ascertain whether passengers really care about waiting-area ambiance.

L. Investigate the possibility of self-insuring all aircraft for any damages to the aircraft itself. Liability insurance would continue to be placed with an insurance company. The banks and leasing companies would require that you deposit $300,000 per aircraft in an escrow account as a reserve against any damage. You would receive interest on this deposit at 2% above prime. You haven't had any hull damage in three years. Hull insurance premiums average $5,000 per year per aircraft.

M. Make a recommendation to the board of directors to accept or reject the offer of a large conglomerate to purchase all the common stock of your airline at 20% above market price. Each member of the management team would receive a "golden parachute" contract that paid $100,000 any officer that was involuntarily separated from the firm. NOTE: The fee for analyzing this proposal is $3,001.

OPTIONAL EXERCISE 1: Passenger Bill of Rights

Most airlines have either been pressured or have done so on their own, created a *Passenger Bill of Rights*. The is usually a short list of the responsibilities the airline has to its customers. It should include everything thing from the rights when a passenger is "bumped" or has a flight canceled, to lost baggage. You may want to search the web sites of airlines for some ideas. You may use a "bulleted list" to keep the document from being too wordy (long winded). Keep the language concise and clear. Write it at the ninth or tenth grade level.

Submit ONE statement <u>per team</u>. Keep a copy for your firm's records.

===

OPTIONAL EXERCISE 2: List of Policies

Most firms have an *Employee Handbook* which describes all employee policies. This assignment will accomplish the same objective except it is to be a concise list (not a book!) of the policies you have for your employees. It should cover everything of importance, including vacations, sick leave, absence without notification, insubordination, promotion policy (promote from within or go outside, and the circumstances for each), child care policy, etc. It is suggested that you use a "bulleted list" to keep the total length reasonable. Write at a level that even an employee without a high school diploma can understand it.

Submit ONE list <u>per team</u>. Keep a copy for your firm's records.

CRITICAL NOTE IF SENDING AND RECEIVING DATA BY EMAIL:

When your instructor sends you the history so that you can print your report, it will come as an attachment to a message. **DO NOT ATTEMPT TO OPEN THIS ATTACHMENT** as it is simply a file with data in it and is NOT a self executable program,(thus the name, DATA1.A3 or whatever).

COPY THIS FILE to either your A: drive or to C:/Airline if you are storing data on your hard drive. Then use the Student simulation program to open the file and print it.

This section contains instructions on loading decisions on the student disk, information to aid you in organizing your team, suggestions for keeping records, and information on how to do a strategic plan and an industry study.

ENTERING DECISIONS ON THE STUDENT DISK

Your instructor may enter your decisions from a decision form that you will submit, or you may be entering decisions on a disk. If you are entering decisions on a disk, this section will apply. The instructor may want your decisions on a (floppy) disk. However, if the instructor is not in your locality, such as in a Web-based course, you will use the decision entry program on the disk and it will create a file containing your decisions. You can then send the instructor the file as an Email attachment.

After your team meets and makes decisions, your next step will be to enter those decisions on your student disk. If the instructor asks you to furnish a disk, do not take chances— purchase a new disk. This will ensure the disk is not problematic. The instructor will need to furnish the student programs for the disk. You may have the Decision Entry Program on your C: drive or on a floppy disk.

Locate the program MENU on the program location. You may use Windows Explorer and double click
   on MENU. Or you may go to START, then RUN, and type
C:\(enter where your programs have been stored)\AirlineStudent (and press Return).
   The file location designation must be exact or you will get a "file not found" error.

Examples of entries on the RUN menu:

A:AirlineStudent.exe
C:\Airline\AirlineStudent.exe   This tells the computer to go to a directory you have created titled
                                   Airline and then run the program *AirlineStudent*

You won't need to type the .exe. It is shown so you will know the entire file name.
In any event, you will need to know your team number, Industry Designation (A to Z), and the number of teams in your industry to continue.

✔ **YOU MUST KNOW THE NUMBER OF TEAMS IN YOUR INDUSTRY BEFORE YOU CAN ENTER DECISIONS.** Ask your instructor for this information.

A menu will appear. Follow the instructions on the screen. You will then begin to enter your decisions in the same order as they appear on the decision form in the back of this manual. Do not panic if you make an error. The program allows you to make corrections all the way through. If you want to modify your decisions after you have left the computer terminal, you must run the entire entry program from the beginning; however, that should be no problem and it will only take a few minutes– a small price to pay for indecision!

If there is a printer attached to your computer, you may make a copy of your decisions to check against what you intended to enter. It is the second item on your menu. If you submit your decisions via disk or file, your instructor will need a copy of your decisions in case there is a problem reading your disk. In most cases, a system (shared) printer may also be used *if the computer is wired to the system printer*.

When you have finished entering your decisions we strongly recommend copying your decision file to another floppy disk. This backup disk should be in the possession of another team member. *Do not* store the disk between the pages in a book or in a hot location such as your car; this can damage the contents.

✖ ✖ **Do not attempt to print your quarterly report at this time (third item on the menu)! The decisions must first be processed by the instructor's computer to compute all the values that are used in the report.** Your instructor may print the quarterly reports for you.

If you are not located at the instructor's location, the history file with quarterly report values will be sent to you via Email attachment.

Sending Decisions via Email or Local Area Network

You may be asked to send your decisions to your instructor via Email. In this case you will attach the decision file that the Decision Entry Program creates to an Email to your instructor. Since each quarter has a different file name, here is the key. The decision file will be named **Team#.IQ** where # is the team number, I is the industry designation, and Q is the quarter number. Thus the file for Team 3, Industry A, and quarter 2 would be **Team3.A2**

Always test your file for a virus before sending it to your instructor. Free virus-checker programs are available on the Internet.

CAUTION! If you send the **Team** (decision) file via Email, make sure your mail browser does not have the option checked that reads something like "Send attachments in the body of the message." The attachment will "open up" when the instructor opens the Email and the decisions will appear in the body of the message in a <u>long string of numbers</u>, unusable by the instructor.

✔ <u>**Always send a copy of your decisions along with the decision file**</u>. This will allow your instructor to enter your decisions in case the file you attached is unreadable by the program.

File Extensions

You will need to read the entire file name if you send files back and forth to your instructor. If you cannot see the .exe at the end of AirlineStudent when you are in Windows Explorer, then you will need to change your Windows settings. The following directions are general in nature so you may need to get help or read the computer manual and/or the Windows manual to ascertain how to reset the file name protocol. The following example is from the Windows 98 instructions. Go to Windows Explorer, then VIEW, then FOLDER OPTIONS, then ADVANCED SETTINGS, then make sure the "Hide File Extensions" box <u>is not</u> checked

Printing the Report with Your Computer

If you are going to print the quarterly report, your instructor will send you a file to do so. It is named **Data#.IQ** where # is the team number, I is the industry designation, and Q is the quarter number.

WHEN YOU TURN YOUR DISK IN TO YOUR INSTRUCTOR, YOU **MUST** TURN IN A COPY OF A COMPLETED DECISION FORM AT THE SAME TIME. This will allow the person processing the disks to check on any decision item that is in doubt, or if the file is corrupt, he or she can re-enter your decisions.

✔ IF YOU DO NOT TURN THE DISK IN AT THE TIME AND PLACE DESIGNATED BY YOUR INSTRUCTOR, or IF YOU DO NOT SUBMIT A DECISION FORM WITH YOUR DISK, <u>YOU WILL BE FINED $10,000!</u> The simulation cannot be processed piecemeal. All student disks must be in to begin the program execution. If your disk is not in, the decisions you made the previous period will automatically be used **without review or modification** by the instructor. Thus, if you

58

made decisions the past period that could damage your firm this new period, tough luck! Once the decisions are processed, there is no way to go back and rerun the period. To do this would change the results of ALL firms since the demand function is interactive.

✔ **Reminder! Decision Files TO the instructor are named TEAM#.IQ and files coming back from the instructor are named DATA#.IQ**

✔ More than one member of the team should keep the files.

✖ **WARNING!** At most universities, one or more computer viruses are present and reside on common area (e.g., computer center) computers. You should ask the computer center staff member whether this is the case and use a virus-detection program to clean your disk before turning it in to your instructor. Viruses can destroy all data on a disk, including your history and decision files.

SAMPLE SCREENS FOR STUDENT DECISION ENTRY PROGRAM

Company 1	DECISION FORM	Quarter 0

* You will have three screens that look similar to your decision form. At the end of each screen, you will have the opportunity to correct any mistakes. You will also have a chance to correct entries after all the items have been entered. **You may re-enter decisions as many times as you wish until you submit your decisions to the instructor.**

* Use a minus sign if item #14 or #15 is a loan payment. Omit commas when entering numbers.

Company 1	DECISION FORM	Quarter No. 0

1.	Fare (in cents; no decimal)	35
2.	Cabin Service (0, 1, 2, 3)	0
3.	Promotion Budget (no comma)	2500
4.	Advertising Budget (no comma)	2500
5.	No. New Salespersons Hired	0
6.	Employee Compensation (0 - 6)	0
7.	Employee Compensation − % increase	0
8.	Quality & Training (no comma)	1000
9.	Maintenance Level (1, 2, 3)	1
10.	Fuel Purchases (0, 1, 2)	0
11.	Cargo Marketing Budget (no comma)	0
12.	Social Responsibility Budget (no comma)	0
13.	Stock Sold in $ (no comma)	500000
14.	Bank Loan/Payment (−)	300000
15.	Long-term Loan/Payment (−)	50000
16.	Dividends Paid (no comma)	5000
17.	Purchase Cert of Deposit	0
	VERIFICATION TOTAL	861036

Do you wish to modify (Y/N)?

Co. 1   Decision Form   Industry A

** Page 2 **

FIRST ACQUISITION TRANSACTION

18.	Number of Aircraft (0-4)	1
19	Type of Aircraft (A-G)	C
20.	Lease(1) or Purchase(2)	1

SECOND ACQUISITION TRANSACTION

21.	Number of Aircraft (0-4)	1
22.	Type of Aircraft (A-G)	D
23.	Lease(1) or Purchase(2)	2
24.	Serial # of disposed A/C	1
25.	Serial # of disposed A/C	0
26.	Serial # of disposed A/C	0
27.	Total Cost of market research $	31000
30.	Incident response	1
	VERIFICATION TOTAL	1007

** Do you wish to modify (Y/N)? **

CHANGES IN MARKETS SERVED (Third Screen in the program)

<u>Enter ONLY the markets you want to change</u>. If abandoning a market, enter zeros for all three entries. If you are changing any items in a market, enter all four items even if only changing one, e.g., market #, # flights, # seats, type of fare sale. When finished, enter no changes at the bottom of the form.

<u>Except in the resort and foreign markets, the minimum number of flights per day is two.</u>

Sample Entries for Company #1

Market Number	Flights per day	Total Seats per day	Fare Sale	Notes
5	0	0	0	Indicates abandoning Market 5
6	3	57	0	Three flights in a 19-seat A/C (Seats = 3 x 19); no fare sale
17	1	30	2	Resort market: One 30-seat flight; Required fare sale 2
19	4	98	1	Two 19-seat flights and two 30-seat flights; fare sale 1

✔ You only need to enter markets which have a change, <u>not all</u> your markets.

✔ If you abandon a market, enter all zeros. Once you have abandoned a market and want to reenter it, you must build the market demand up again. There is not carry over effect.

READ AGAIN THE IMPORTANT TEXT BOX ON PAGE 56!

ORGANIZING YOUR TEAM

Key Personnel Assignments

Your team should discuss the various strengths of its members and the academic and work background of each. This will allow each team member to assume a position in the airline that matches his or her experience and/or knowledge. The organization chart below indicates some of the key positions one might find in a small commuter airline.

<u>Suggested</u> <u>Duties</u>

President	Overall coordination, encouragement, peacemaking, strategic planning; sets lead times, and ensures that deadlines are met.
Vice-President of Finance	Financial analysis and control; lease/buy analysis; recommends fuel and financial decisions (loans/CDs).
Vice-President of Marketing	Recommends marketing budget, cabin service, research studies, and fares; analyzes strategies of competitors.
Vice-President of Operations and Human Resources	Recommends compensation, quality and training budgets, number of flights and seats; crew training and retention; tracks reliability trends.
Vice-President of Planning	Analyzes all markets and service to those markets; recommends new routes and changes in current routes, aircraft procurement and disposal from maintenance point of view.
Vice-President of Maintenance	Recommends maintenance level and fuel purchases.

If there are fewer than six people on your team, you will need to double up on some of the duties. In particular, the president may want to assume the duties of the planner, and the operations VP assume the maintenance duties. In a simulation, the president DOES NOT have veto power or the "final word." Of course, your team may make any rules it wishes, but if the president is too heavy-handed, everyone else may quit!

The president should be chosen carefully! Choose someone who can provide the team with time discipline and keep everyone working. The president must take the lead in planning meetings, delegating work assignments, and handling other leadership duties. If the president is not working out, the team may gently suggest a change! If someone tries any position and does not like it, the team should be open to switching positions. In fact, if the accountant in the group takes the role of financier, others won't learn some of the areas of accounting and finance that may come in very useful later in their careers.

AIRLINE is a highly sophisticated interactive simulation and should not be taken lightly by your team. Success in the game, both in terms of the learning experience and company profits, is directly related to the degree of organization and cooperation among company (team) members. Game results are directly correlated to well-thought-out analysis and strategic planning in the decision process. An early and complete familiarization with the contents of the student manual will increase the chances of success; knowledge of the proper use of analysis forms (or the same work accomplished on a personal computer spreadsheet) is imperative if one is to stay abreast of the game.

Record Keeping

Your instructor will tell you which of the following organizational assignments will be required:

1. Prepare an organization chart to include your team members' names and include what you think would be the next lower level of personnel on your chart (i.e., who would report to each of your officers).

2. Corporate Strategic Planning
   Each company should prepare its objectives and goals; implementation strategy; and operating plans and procedures for the firm. There is a suggested format for this assignment in this section of the manual.

3. Company Logbook
   Each company should keep a logbook of the important data accumulated while playing the simulation. Logbooks are analogous to the written records that firms maintain during the course of normal operations. All data, information, charts, copies of forms that were turned in, graphs, and narratives should be included. Your instructor will inform you whether this is to be turned in at the end of the simulation or be available during class periods for spot checks.

4. Comparative Charts and Graphs
   It is often very helpful to have historical information organized so managers can spot early trends and trouble spots. The following list is not all-inclusive but is offered as a reference point of departure:

   a. Cash position each quarter
   b. Mileage flown as a percentage of maximum mileage available
   c. Fare and industry average
   d. Earnings, dividends paid, and stock price
   e. Sales forecast and actual sales (by total passengers, dollar sales, and revenue passenger miles)
   f. Passenger load factor (this is a key indicator of success)
   g. Yield per revenue passenger mile, cost per available seat mile, and yield per available seat mile
   h. Employee compensation, training expenditures, and turnover
   i. Various expense categories should be carefully monitored against some meaningful performance standard. Examples include: maintenance cost per mile flown or passenger service cost per passenger handled; marketing expense per sales dollar; administrative expense per passenger or per revenue passenger mile.
   j. Tracking competitor behavior in markets served can be extremely useful information.
   k. Seats sold in each market as a percentage of the total (this requires purchasing the relevant market research study)
   l. Quality expenditures and quality index
   m. Various standard financial ratios. There are forms provided for this in the manual.

Minutes of Company Meetings

Your instructor will tell you whether this is a requirement and whether it is to be handed in with the decisions or kept in the company logbook. In either case, the minutes should be recorded WHEN THE MEETING OCCURS, not re-created from recall later.

The minutes do not need to be written following Roberts Rules of Order but rather should indicate the rationale of the KEY decisions that were made; minority views should be indicated as well as those of the majority. Any discussion that may be considered relevant should be recorded; in all cases major decisions and the rationale behind those decisions should be recorded. Examples include: fare changes; aircraft purchases and why a certain type of aircraft was chosen; changes in cabin service; major shifts in advertising, promotion, or training budgets; major changes in employee compensation and why one alternative was chosen over others; which method of acquiring and financing new aircraft was chosen and why (lease or buy, bank loan or stock issue).

There are forms at the end of this section (titled Airline Simulation Decision Log) that can be used to record your meetings.

THE STRATEGIC PLANNING PROCESS

Planning is the process of preparing for the future. While thoughtful and detailed planning does not ensure success, the vast majority of successful organizations practice good planning and strategic analysis. Of course, a firm can do too much detailed planning and not be flexible enough to react to environmental changes and opportunities. On the other hand, operating without a plan also has its drawbacks; if an organization doesn't know where it's going, how will it know when it gets there? There is a hierarchy to the planning process—from the broad and general direction set by top management to the detailed planning required at the operating level. The outline below indicates this process.

    I.   Establish the Purpose (mission, master strategy) of the Organization

   II.   Analyze the Firm's Environment

        A. The External Environment (termed industry study)
           1. Environmental Threats
           2. Environmental Opportunities

        B. The Internal Environment
           1. Organizational Strengths
           2. Organizational Weaknesses

  III.   List all Possible Courses of Action

  IV.   Select Best Course(s) of Action

   V.   Establish Goals and Objectives That Will Accomplish the Desired Course of Action

  VI.   Prepare an Action or Strategic Plan that Describes *How* the Objectives Will be Accomplished

 VII.   Establish Policies, Standard Operating Procedures, and Methods That Will Expedite the Accomplishment of the Objectives

VIII.   Establish a Control and Feedback System to Keep the Organization on Track With the Strategic Plan

In narrative form, the outline above answers these questions:

- Where are we now?
- Where could we go? What could we do?
- What is the best thing for us to do?
- How are we going to do it? Who is going to do what parts?
- How are we going to measure our progress?

ESTABLISHING GOALS AND OBJECTIVES

Textbooks in the strategic management area define key terms that are used somewhat differently. We are using a generic approach to strategic planning; however, your instructor may prefer a different method or format than the one suggested. Here are some definitions that may be useful:

PURPOSE (Mission or Master Strategy): Denotes what the firm should be doing and why it exists. It answers the question "What business are we in?" in terms of market needs.

GOALS OR OBJECTIVES: Specifies what the firm is striving for, what it wants to achieve. It is highly desirable that targets be established that are quantifiable and measurable.

There are ten areas for which objectives should be established:

1. Market Standing
2. Productivity
3. Worker Performance
4. Physical Facilities
5. Stockholder Responsibility
6. Profitability
7. Innovation
8. Manager Performance and Development
9. Public (or Social) Responsibility
10. Financial Targets

STRATEGIES: A description of HOW the firm intends to achieve its objectives, i.e., a detailed Action plan.

POLICIES, PROCEDURES, METHODS: Detailed plans that govern decisions at the operating level to expedite decision making and implementation.

An Example of a Simple Strategic Plan

Purpose or *Mission*: To transport cargo by air.

One *Objective* could be: To attain a 20% market share in 10 markets within 18 months.

A *Strategy* to implement this objective: To increase the sales force to two full-time salespersons and to increase advertising by 25%.

A *Policy*: To fly the first 200 pounds of cargo for a new customer free.

A *Standard Procedure*: Upon receipt of a new customer contract,
   1. The salesperson will ascertain that all details and agreements are executable.
   2. A credit check will be made before the goods are shipped.

The format on the next page may be useful to your team in its strategic planning.

FORMAT FOR A STRATEGIC PLAN

The following format may be used as a guide for preparing your strategic plan.

I. The Internal Environment
List the strengths and weaknesses of the organization. Areas include: relations with and strengths in dealing with competitors, customers, employees, and suppliers; financial strength; physical facilities and equipment; employee and manager expertise, morale, and training.

II. The External Environment
   a. List the opportunities and threats found in the environment
   b. List the specific factors in the external environment that pertain to this industry and company. Examples include:

   Social Forces; Social Structure and Change
   Political Influences and Forces
   The Legal Environment and Governmental Regulations
   Economic Factors and Trends
   Energy and Raw Material Costs
   Technological Development and Change
   Industry Atmosphere and Trends
   Competitive Structure, Atmosphere, and Trends
   Consumer Desires, Changes, and Values
   Financial Environment

   Some authors refer to the analysis above as an environmental scan. It answers the question, "Where are we now?" and establishes the foundation for looking toward the future in preparing goals and objectives. The outline below can be used for the remainder of the strategic plan.

III. Overall Purpose or Mission

IV. Objective or Goal

V. The Action or Strategic Plan for implementing the objective or goal

VI. Policies to aid in implementing this objective or goal

VII. Standard procedures, methods, or operating plans that need to be established to implement the objective/goal

VIII. Methods of control and feedback

ANALYZING AN INDUSTRY

Analyzing the industry in which one is doing strategic planning is an important aspect of gathering data on the firm's external environment. While all libraries have secondary sources for obtaining industrial information, primary sources, such as interviewing an official in the industry, would be extremely valuable to the business student. An outline for an industry study is shown next.

1. History of the Industry
    Changes, trends, and responses to challenges.

2. Analyze Forces Within the Industry
    Consumer wants and needs, socioeconomic trends affecting the industry, technological changes and directions, governmental regulations/trends, resource availability, challenges of substitute products/services, ease of entry and trends of new entrants.

3. Competitive Structure
    Determine whether the industry is monopolistic, oligopolistic, highly competitive, etc. Determine the size and strength of firms in the industry (a few very large, one or two large and the balance small, etc.). Assess the industry leaders and followers.

4. Evaluate Resources Required and Availability
    Consider financial, physical, and raw materials resources; make future projections.

5. Industry Marketing Trends
    What constitutes the normal marketing mix, i.e., how is the product or service generally sold? Analyze trends in advertising, promotions, prices, promotional pricing, as well as the importance of other organizations to the industry, such as trade organizations, lobbying groups, and other industries.

6. Industry Opportunities
    Consider new businesses you might enter, demographic and technological changes that may increase the potential for new product lines or service businesses, etc.

7. Industry Threats
    Demographic or socioeconomic changes that are a threat, increased government intervention or regulation, substitute products, spiraling costs causing prices to increase, thereby decreasing the potential market.
    Availability of raw materials or supportive goods or services. If the industry is based on serving another industry, what is the economic health of the supported industry?

8. Forecasts of Future Changes
    What may change? What effect would that have on the business?
    What activities could you engage in that would result in a positive change (such as lobbying)?
    Consider doing a "What If" analysis for certain crucial changes.

AIRLINE SIMULATION DECISION LOG   Industry ___   Qtr# ___   Co # ____

Reproduce as many copies of this form as needed.

State any major change in your overall strategy (e.g., long-term objectives) and how it differs from the original. [For quarter 1 please state your overall strategy.]

_____

_____

_____

_____

_____

State the major issues and/or problems to be discussed at the meeting:

_____

_____

_____

_____

_____

_____

List each MAJOR decision or change in previous operating policy you are going to make this quarter and give the rationale behind the decision:

_____

_____

_____

_____

_____

_____

_____

_____

_____

_____

_____

(Use additional pages if required)

Members of the team present at this meeting on_____ of_____

_____   _____

_____   _____

_____   _____

This section contains forms for completing a management audit, stockholders meeting, and peer evaluation.

MANAGEMENT AUDIT (If assigned by your instructor)

Your team should be prepared to make a short (8 to 10 minute) presentation to the class. Your instructor may also want a written report; if so, the report should be typed and be well organized. Make sure you turn in any additional analyses you performed in order to make better decisions, including charts, graphs, etc., for which you have not received credit. You may want to prepare a short handout for the class, indicating the main points of your report.

For the purpose of this audit, assume that your firm is a case study out of the textbook! Investigate the performance of the firm as though you were management consultants brought in to determine what kind of job the management team of the firm has done. Of course, there are several methods of approaching this assignment and you are encouraged to be creative. The major point you will be graded on is your OBJECTIVITY AND HONESTY in reporting your findings; i.e., be brutally frank! Your instructor has been following all the teams closely via administrator records furnished by the computer, and any attempt to "whitewash" or omit critical points will be dealt with unkindly. Listed below are some key questions to help you get your thinking caps on. However, your report (both verbal and written) may follow any CREATIVE format you wish; just try to address in some way or other most of the points covered below.

Your instructor may ask you to conduct the audit by playing the role of a consultant firm. This will encourage objectivity on your part.

1. Refer to the original goals and objectives. Did the strategies work as planned? What strategies, goals, objectives, policies, etc., were changed? Why?
   How closely did the firm end up doing what it said it was going to do?
   (Your team will not be penalized on this point if your goals did change substantially. Just be honest.)

2. The functions of the manager are planning, organizing, directing work, and controlling.
   To what extent and how were these functions handled by this team? Comment particularly on the controls that you may or may not have used. Were they effective?
   Did the team have enough records, controls, and worksheets to manage effectively?

3. If this firm were to begin again, what should it do differently?

4. If the management team were going to be transferred, what advice should it give to the new team coming in to manage this company?

5. Does the firm have a prudent dividend policy? What would a committee of stockholders say about this firm's treatment of its stockholders?

6. Did the team make decisions on a rational basis or did it often "stab in the dark?"

7. What are the firm's strengths and weaknesses?
   What are the threats and opportunities facing the firm at this time?

8. At this point, is the firm a healthy, going concern? Is there any evidence of "end playing" the simulation? Such evidence would include a large dividend payment at the end, reducing all budgets, buying or selling stock to influence the stock price, etc.

9. Was there any evidence of lack of teamwork in the firm? If so, what communication, decision-making, and cooperation efforts need improving?

One of the peer audit forms on pages 75 and 77 is usually completed after the last decision period and submitted to the instructor. This MUST be done without consultation with other team members. Your instructor will tell you which form to use.

> **IMPORTANT NOTE:** Most instructors will penalize a team heavily if the team does anything at the end of the simulation that attempts to make the firm look better. See number 8 above.

ANNUAL REPORT AND STOCKHOLDERS' MEETING
(If assigned by your instructor)

Corporations report the state of the organization to their owners (stockholders) on an annual basis. Sometime after your first year of operations, you may be asked to conduct an annual meeting with the class acting as your stockholders. The actual length and format of the oral presentation will be assigned by your instructor. The annual meeting is used to communicate the condition of the corporation to the owners and is a public relations vehicle for the general public, investment bankers, and prospective stock purchasers. [Hint: Do not feel you must "tell all" and reveal all your future plans in detail. Likewise, you may merge certain expenses on the financial statements you prepare, e.g., under marketing expenses you could include promotions budget, advertising, marketing research, and salespersons expenses.

Each team will be expected to prepare a short Annual Report for its stockholders and reproduce sufficient copies for each of the other teams and the instructor. You should check the annual report section in the library to get a more complete idea concerning what should be included. Some items that the firm should include in the written portion are: a brief synopsis of sales and earnings trends; an explanation of start-up problems and how they are being overcome; a general statement of the financial health of the firm; and a discussion of dividend plans and policy, expansion plans, future prospects, etc.

In addition to this brief narrative of operations, you will need to include the financial report for your firm. The financial report includes, at a minimum, an income statement, balance sheet, statement of changes in financial conditions, and explanations that include comparisons to prior-year data. This listing is not meant to limit other financial information you may want to include in your report. Since all financial reports use the previous year with which to compare current performance, use the beginning balance sheet for Quarter 0 (see page 28). For an annual Profit and Loss statement, multiply the quarter 0 sales and expenses times 4 to obtain a full year of profit and loss information for the previous year.

Each member of each team is responsible for analyzing the annual reports of the other teams and asking questions during the presentations.

This form should be completed and handed in to the instructor no later than _____. Note: Exclude in any numerical reporting any instances that were the fault of the computer or the administrator.

1. How many times did the team have a zero cash balance (overdraft loan)? _____

2. How many times was there an excess amount of cash that was not invested in CDs (excessive is defined as over $300,000)? _____

3. How many quarters did you have aircraft utilization of less than 95%? (from the Mileage Analysis form) _____

4. Total dividends paid: $_____. Total amount per share: _____
   List the quarters in which you made a dividend payment and amounts (per share) of that payment:

5. In view of your dividend record above, do you think you were fair with the owners (stockholders) of the firm? Why or why not?

6. How many markets did you abandon during the simulation? _____
   If you abandoned a market and re-entered it, count it! Why did you abandon the markets, if any were abandoned?

7. Total amount spent on market research for the entire simulation: $_____
   Do you think this was sufficient? Too much?

8. What was Average Passenger Load Factor (for entire simulation)? _____%

9. Total passengers flown (for the entire simulation): _____

10. What are your total profits after taxes but before dividends since quarter 0? $ _____

11. Profit per passenger flown for all quarters being reported (total profits before dividends divided by total passengers for all quarters): $ _____

12. Return on sales for the entire simulation (total profits after taxes but before dividends, divided by total revenues): _____%

12. Return on sales for the entire simulation (total profits before dividends divided by total revenues): _____%

13. Return on equity for entire simulation (total profits before taxes divided by average total equity): _____%

14. What was your average stock price for the entire simulation? ____.___

15. What was your reliability at the end of the simulation? _____%

16. What was your employee turnover at the end of the simulation? _____%

17. How many quarters did you exceed the maximum mileage? _____

18. List your fare for each quarter:

Quarter		Quarter	
1	_____	7	_____
2	_____	8	_____
3	_____	9	_____
4	_____	10	_____
5	_____	11	_____
6	_____	12	_____

19. Indicate any other negative factors (weaknesses) that are relevant to this audit of your airline:

20. Indicate any other positive factors (strengths) that are relevant to this audit of your airline:

BUSINESS SIMULATION PEER EVALUATION
(End-of-Semester)

The purpose of this analysis is to give credit to those students who went the "extra mile" or who did their fair share of the simulation work. Conversely, if any team members did not do their fair share (for whatever reason) then they should not get full credit for the simulation work. Be assured that all data on this form will be held in confidence.

PERFORMANCE EVALUATION IS AN IMPORTANT PART OF EVERY MANAGER'S JOB; YOU'RE EXPECTED TO MAKE A FAIR AND ACCURATE EVALUATION.

KEY TO NUMERICAL RANKING

ATTENDANCE & COOPERATION:
5 = Was a team leader both in and outside class; cooperation superior
4 = Attended meetings regularly; good cooperation; a team player
3 = Attended meetings fairly regularly; did what was asked but no more
2 = Missed some meetings and did the minimum amount of work
1 = Poor attendance at meetings and/or poor cooperation/workload

ACADEMIC CONTRIBUTION:
5 = A team leader in ideas; enthusiastic; had a lot of good ideas
4 = Contributed greatly to the team; did more than his/her fair share
3 = Had good ideas from time to time; an average performance
2 = Probably was either too quiet or not sufficiently interested to be an effective academic contributor to the team
1 = Contributed little to the team

TEAM PLAYER:
5 = THE TEAM LEADER (**only one or two persons may receive a score of 5**)
4 = A team player, second to the leader only slightly (two people may be assigned this score if they were co-leaders)
3 = An average member of the team; good work
2 = Slightly below average member of the team
1 = Contributed the least to the team

Your Name _____ (DO NOT SCORE YOURSELF)

NAME	Attendance & Cooperation (5, 4, 3, 2, 1)		Academic Contribution (5, 4, 3, 2, 1)		Team Player (5, 4, 3, 2, 1)		Total Points (0 to 15)
_____	_____	+	_____	+	_____	=	_____
_____	_____	+	_____	+	_____	=	_____
_____	_____	+	_____	+	_____	=	_____
_____	_____	+	_____	+	_____	=	_____
_____	_____	+	_____	+	_____	=	_____
_____	_____	+	_____	+	_____	=	_____
_____	_____	+	_____	+	_____	=	_____

>> Add the points from the three columns and place in TOTAL POINTS column.

EXECUTIVE BONUS RECOMMENDATION Form 3
(Peer Evaluation normally used at mid-semester)

As a member of your firm's Executive Compensation Committee, you have been assigned the task of allocating $40,000 among the managers of your firm.

NOTE: A fair, firm, and objective performance evaluation is a crucial function of the manager. While peer evaluation is not an easy task, your instructor expects you to complete this task honestly.

	Fill in names of the executives of your firm, including your own	Fill in the Amount of the Executive Bonus
YOUR NAME >>>	_____	$_____
	_____	$_____
	_____	$_____
	_____	$_____
	_____	$_____
	_____	$_____
	_____	$_____
	_____	$_____
	TOTAL	**$ 40,000**

DEBRIEFING QUESTIONNAIRE   **AIRLINE SIMULATION**

Check with your instructor to ascertain if this is to be anonymous.

Your Name_____ Industry_____ Company #___

1. What did you like about the simulation?

2. What didn't you like about the simulation?

3. To what extent did the simulation help you understand the operation of an organization from the viewpoint of top management?

4. An objective of a simulation is to help participants understand the TOTAL firm and interrelationships between the different functional areas. To what extent did the simulation achieve this objective?

5. To what extent did the simulation help sharpen your ability to analyze problems and recommend solutions (i.e., decision-making skills)?

6. What other skills did you learn because of the simulation and group decision making that occurred?

7. How many hours per decision period did your team meet as a team (either face-to-face, by phone, or via Internet: _____ hours at the beginning _____ hours after Quarter 4

8. How many hours per decision period SHOULD a team meet to make decisions? _____

9. How many hours per decision period did YOU spend (excluding team meetings) in preparing for the team meeting or in doing outside work, gathering data, analyzing data, working with a spreadsheet program, etc.? _____

-over-

10. Please make any comments you feel (pro and con) about any of the incidents:

11. Please make any comments you feel (pro and con) about any other part of the simulation:

12. Do you have any other suggestions concerning the simulation or the method in which the instructor handled it?

13. Suppose that another student told you she was going to take this course next semester. She has the choice between a course that has case studies only and a course like this one that has a business simulation. What would be your advice about the course choice?

14. What would be your advice to her about the simulation if she were to take the course with the simulation?

15. Do you feel the simulation is a valuable learning experience? Why?

This section presents the case of a firm that is about the same size and condition of the firm your team will manage in the simulation. Analyzing the airline industry and this case will help prepare your team for the internal and external environmental factors in the simulation. Note: This case was written after extensive research into an actual commuter airline.

HISTORY OF THE AIRLINE

Mid-Continent is well known to thousands of people living in small communities scattered throughout the Great Lakes region. Like other commuter airlines, the company has been providing air service to cities and towns that were unattractive to large carriers because of the population size or the limited facilities at the local airport.

In 1978, the Federal government deregulated the entire airline industry, leaving all companies able to compete for passengers by creating competitive fare structures and competitive routes. One response by major carriers was to diminish service to the less profitable markets and create hubs in large cities. Commuter airlines jumped in to fill the service vacuums left in many medium-sized and small cities.

This airline was established as a "mom and pop" business by the fixed-base operator in a North Central state to fill the void left when North Central Airlines abandoned the area. The airline grew from a fledgling carrier that transported 2,710 passengers in its first year, to a regional airline that was carrying 90,000 passengers in 2000. The airline has had a cyclical history of profitability, ranging from small losses to small profits. Loads have been from 4 to 15 passengers per flight. (Nine passengers is slightly above a breakeven load.) The present fleet consists of three 19--passenger Beechcraft 1900s.

As a member of the Airline Reporting Corporation (ARC) and by virtue of bilateral agreements with major carriers, Mid-Continent currently has interline ticketing and baggage arrangements with all major carriers. The agreement allows Mid-Continent to issue tickets to any destination at competitive rates and to offer the convenience of baggage checked through to the final destination. Increased sophistication in equipment has increased dependability.

The designations "commuter" and "regional" have become synonymous, as the small airlines fill gaps left by large carriers and create their own mini-hub operations in medium-sized cities that have lost their major airline service.

COMMUTER AIRLINE EQUIPMENT

Mid-Continent often competes with other commuters as well as some national airlines for modest numbers of passengers departing from a location. This smaller market is reflected in the type of equipment flown. The available aircraft range in size from 15-passenger prop jets to 50-passenger fan jets. Although some of the equipment dates back to the 1950's, newly developed commuter aircraft contain state-of-the-art technology in materials, fuel efficiency, noise abatement, jet engines (with and without propellers), and nonflammable cabin materials. Since there is an abundance of preowned equipment available as other, larger and more profitable airlines "traded up," the airline has a large choice of aircraft to choose from *if the managers decide to expand.*

The composition of the fleet of any airline may reflect corporate strategy. Since there is no perfect aircraft for all markets, airlines have the discretion of selecting from a wide variety of aircraft types. Although aircraft selection has an impact on demand, the potential increase in revenue-passenger miles flown in the "perfect aircraft" can be offset by higher costs as the maintenance department has to stock more parts and train mechanics to work on a larger variety of aircraft; pilot training costs are increased as well.

Passengers have a definite preference for cabin-class service (i.e., flight attendants and stand-up headroom), and a slight preference for jet aircraft (versus prop jets, which are in wide service). The revenues generated may be offset by the higher cost of equipment, speed, fuel efficiency, or other variables that affect the cost of operating the equipment. Thus, a successful commuter/regional airline may have a fleet that includes a potpourri of equipment, including smaller craft. See Table 4 on page 13 for aircraft descriptions and costs.

FARES

Airline fares are one of the more complex pricing systems in the free enterprise world. All airlines post a standard fare for each portion of a route in the Department of Transportation listings; this is known as the "Y" fare. These fares are set artificially high and are used as a baseline for discounts and to calculate portions of tickets that are issued in conjunction with other airlines. In addition, airlines develop promotional fare packages from time to time to introduce new service or promote sluggish demand. Promotional fares stimulate demand but reduce revenues. The competitive market is very reactive to fare changes; thus fare reductions tend to be copied by competitors and the benefits to a single airline are short-lived.

TICKETING

Although many airlines maintain independent ticketing services, approximately 75% of the tickets sold for Mid-Continent are booked through travel agents. The fee for this service averages 10% of the ticket price, and therefore it is common practice to forecast net revenues at an amount that is 90% of the sales forecast for the coming financial period.

In recent years, several of the major airlines have developed computer reservation services (CRS). Since the mid-1970s, the ease of using the listings made them popular with travel agents. Since travel agents are the main source of sales, Mid-Continent Airlines subscribed to these listings. This imposed additional variable costs per ticket of approximately 1%. Lately, many firms on the Internet have entered the business of selling airline tickets and packages.

ROUTING

Airlines such as Mid-Continent generally fly routes that terminate in larger cities that have major airline connections. Passengers prefer nonstop flights at convenient times and this factor can stimulate demand. However, since the demand may be small at any particular stop, commuter and regional airlines will often provide direct service (on the same plane) to a hub city, making one or more stops along the way. (*Direct service* means no aircraft change, although the aircraft may make a stop or two.) Mid-Continent managers have these strategic options:

1. They may choose to stay totally independent of larger airlines and issue separate tickets.

2. They may have *interline* agreements with larger airlines for connecting routes to other cities not served by Mid-Continent.

3. They may actually use the designator or symbol of the larger airline, paint their airplanes to show the other carrier's logo and colors, and establish a formal arrangement to feed the major

carrier's routes (e.g., the Delta Connection, United Express). This is termed "dual designating" and many small airlines have found it to be the key to survival.

Each strategy has an impact on demand and the level of revenue from a portion of a flight. The independent ticketing approach may yield the largest per capita revenue for each ticket issued but prohibits through-ticketing, thus limiting the potential market. An interlining agreement provides through-ticket and baggage service but decreases the portion of the fare received by the commuter airline. Dual designation with a major airline makes the commuter airline appear to be part of the larger network. However, the commuter/regional airline pays a fee ranging from 5% to 10% per passenger boarded and sacrifices much scheduling autonomy.

Airplanes do not generate revenues when they sit on the ground. Therefore, utilization is a variable that can affect successful operations. A typical aircraft can be flown for 12 to 14 hours a day, which allows for overnight maintenance and an average of 10 to 12 legs per day. This calculates at 1,800 miles flown per day for the airline's aircraft.

REGULATORY ENVIRONMENT

Despite the 1978 deregulation of fares and routes, Mid-Continent and the industry as a whole tend to be heavily regulated in several areas. Minimum equipment maintenance schedules are specified and monitored by government agencies. This requires extensive record keeping. In addition, some airlines choose a maintenance program in excess of Federal requirements to decrease unplanned, out-of-service time and to increase safety. The extra maintenance provides the same marginal benefits to the company that an insurance policy might; it is difficult to determine the most cost-effective level. Minimum levels of pilot training are mandatory and become a cost of doing business. Some airlines provide training beyond the minimum level to increase pilot effectiveness. However, those commuter/regional airlines that provide extensive training lose a greater portion of their pilots to larger airlines.

Aircraft that have more than 30 seats require a special certification by the FAA; moreover, they are required to have a flight attendant. The paperwork to document compliance with these regulations can result in increased staff size. Compliance with regulating agencies is costly to the airlines in terms of the staff needed, the paperwork required, and the direct costs incurred.

FINANCING ASSETS

Mid-Continent Airlines has several types of fixed assets: airplanes, ground equipment (i.e., ground power units, tugs, de-icing equipment, baggage carts, and trucks), maintenance hangars, office facilities, and computers. In addition, preventive and corrective maintenance require an inventory of spare parts that may include extra engines. This inventory can tie up significant amounts of cash. Some fluctuation occurs based on the size and the composition of the fleet.

Assets are financed through several channels. Aircraft may be leased for a period of time ranging from 4 to 15 years. Leasing provides advantages to an airline that does not have cash available for a loan down payment, does not have sufficient collateral, or wants to use a specific type of equipment for a limited period of time. Airplane leases may be either operating or capital leases. Operating leases do not appear as assets on the balance sheet and do not increase the value of the company to its owners. A capital lease appears as an asset and as a long-term liability on the financial statements.

A second financial market available to the airlines is the conventional loan. Loans require down payments plus some assurances to the lender (collateral) that the payments can be made. The typical loan period is 10 to 12 years. Airline equipment may also be financed by a stock issue. The risks in acquiring all of the necessary funds are higher but a well-managed company may be able to finance purchases for a lower cost of capital by issuing stock.

Fledgling airlines frequently need a line of credit to finance current assets and meet ongoing expenses (working capital). This is usually handled by a line of credit (demand notes) that ranges upward from 2% over the prime interest rate. As with other businesses, an inability to meet current expenses can be the downfall of an otherwise solvent commuter/regional airline.

HUMAN RESOURCE DEVELOPMENT

Currently, Mid-Continent has 81 employees. Because of its small size, the salaries and wages of employees have been below the market for airline employees of national and major airlines. Station personnel are frequently paid minimum wage; this salary differential holds true for pilots and ground crews. Thus, they have become a training ground for the larger airlines, with relatively high employee turnover (15% or more) causing additional expense to the airline.

Strategies used by other regional airlines to counteract this problem:

a. Encourage a sense of ownership in the company through stock options and profit-sharing. Employees are called "managers" of the position they hold (e.g., a ticket agent becomes a customer service manager).

c. Job design of ground crews includes rotation through several types of positions.

d. Development of clearly defined career paths.

The relationship between salaries and turnover is not clear, since the major airlines are thought to have higher status. This may diminish the effect of increased remuneration. Mid-Continent has been passive about the turnover problem and views it as a cost of doing business. In some small cities, the airline's success in ground crew and station personnel retention has been a function of the available job markets in those locations.

ORGANIZATION

Mid-Continent is organized into five small departments: operations, flight, maintenance, passenger service, and administration. There is little overlap between the areas, and employees must have specialized training as required by regulatory agencies.

All functions, including marketing, ticketing, and computer information services, are handled by these departments. Creating an efficient organization is difficult for Mid-Continent and other small operators, as well as costly in terms of personnel.

Those airlines that are dual designators with major airlines may receive services such as ground operations or computer information systems as part of the agreement. Remaining autonomous is costly to Mid-Continent in terms of organizational design as well as in attracting passengers.

The organization chart for Mid-Continent appears on the next page.

MID-CONTINENT ORGANIZATION CHART

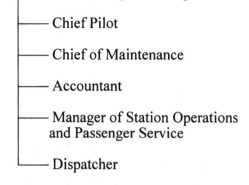

PRESIDENT (also pilots a flight when necessary)

- Chief Pilot
- Chief of Maintenance
- Accountant
- Manager of Station Operations and Passenger Service
- Dispatcher

GROUND OPERATIONS

A significant cost to airlines is the operation of "stations" in the airports. The station provides the boarding, baggage handling, and ground services to the passengers and aircraft; thus, both corporate image and competence are important issues. A commuter or regional airline may choose to establish its own station or may subcontract for space and staff from another airline.

Opening an autonomous station is expensive, due to rentals and staffing. However, the company can usually maintain better control of the passenger and flight-operation activities with its own policies and procedures for ticketing and handling of station equipment. The station can also enhance the image and visibility of the airline. Contracting for gate services (ticketing, food, and fuel) from another carrier provides quick start-up and minimal costs of operation. However, the other carrier's employees are not subject to the jurisdiction of the contracting airline; this may create problems for the airline, its equipment, and passengers. Mid-Continent uses both contract services and its own stations, depending on the assessment of potential demand from the location. Opening its own counter costs at least $10,000; contracting for a station costs $3,000 to $4,000 monthly rent plus promotional expenses.

CONCLUSION

In 2002, the owners of Mid-Continent felt that they were at a crossroads. They had just received an offer of a loan of $500,000 that would greatly bolster working capital and make it possible to increase their three-plane fleet by leasing additional equipment.

Deregulation had opened many possible markets and airlines such as Air Wisconsin had made moves to fill the void created as the larger carriers pulled out of the smaller markets. The loan was being offered at 12% annual interest; the duration was to be six years. Mid-Continent was required to use all existing assets as collateral. In addition, the lender was to receive 30% of the common stock of the corporation. While the owners did not like the idea of giving up some of the ownership of the firm, they felt they could not get traditional bank financing because of their inadequate earnings record.

However, a second possibility had also arisen. A large holding company had offered to purchase the airline for the book value of $1,737,182 plus $250,000. This was an interesting offer to the owners, as they could "walk away" from the business with a moderate nest egg. They felt that *if* they were going to sell, it was a fair offer in light of the poor earnings record of the airline.

The decision was important enough to get some advice from a consultant, Dr. Peggy Golden, who was a certified pilot and had been the CEO of a small but successful commuter operation. After several days of studying the situation, Dr. Golden met with Jerald Smith, president of Mid-Continent, to report her findings.

The Options

"I have studied your flight operations, finances, and marketing strategies and can find strengths and weaknesses in each area. My greatest concern is that your aircraft are not the best type for the 600 (round trip) mile markets and that you are not taking advantage of some markets that are wide open," commented Dr. Golden.

Smith replied, "I am aware of this but the FAA has had us under scrutiny lately. Our oldest Beech needs updated instruments and radios. In addition, one aircraft is 18 years old and all were purchased used. The oldest one is beginning to be more costly to maintain at this point. You can see how maintenance problems with their associated costs and the weather have kept us from flying at an optimal level. We have cash problems that are exacerbated by overhead costs. We need a certain level of support personnel to maintain a three-aircraft fleet; however, we could add two more aircraft at no additional overhead cost."

The president continued, "There are markets that are not currently being served in our area and I think we could lease a couple of new aircraft. But it takes from 6 to 12 months to get to the breakeven point in a new market, and we just don't have the working capital for that. I suppose if we tightened our belts and tried to get some short-term credit at a couple of banks in the small cities we serve, we could do it. We can't grow because of our slim profits, and because we can't grow we can't improve our profit picture. It seems like a vicious circle!"

"I have evaluated the two options that are available to you," said Dr. Golden. "The $500,000 loan has the potential to provide enough cash to improve your maintenance program and add a substantial amount to your working capital. This would make your firm much more attractive to a leasing company and you would be able to lease some additional aircraft. In fact, there are aircraft manufacturers have gotten very aggressive lately in order to sell pre-owned aircraft that have been traded in for new planes; I think they would be able to offer you good leases. Right now the going rate for a pre-owned, newly refurbished British Aero 31 is $2.2 million and the monthly lease is $82,000."

Smith responded thoughtfully, "Yes, that five hundred grand would sure get us out of the hole and we would be able to take advantage of some the markets that are opening up. However, giving up 30% of the common stock just sticks in our craw a bit. But I guess if I were lending this shoestring airline money, I'd feel the same way. So, what do you think about the offer from the holding company?"

"I have to admit that the offer is very fair," the consultant stated. "It would give you an opportunity to walk out free of any debt. The holding company wants to keep Mid-Continent flying, since it is the only airline serving their home-office city. You would have the satisfaction of knowing that your years of hard work were not in vain and the name Mid-Continent would continue."

"If we keep the airline, what kind of strategies would you suggest?" asked the president.

Golden responded, "The possible strategies are about the same regardless of who owns the airline. The crucial thing is to maximize the use of your equipment and serve markets that will provide you with greater than a breakeven load. You may have to give up some markets to which you have an emotional attachment because you have served them for such a long time."

"The airline can remain small and the owners can have fun and some sense of satisfaction out of it. You are both in your mid-50s and in excellent health. You do have a positive cash flow and are making a decent living. On the other hand, there is potential for growth in this industry at this time. If the airline expands, the organization will have to change in order to accommodate this new strategy; this would adhere to the strategic-planning principle of creating a structure that aids in implementing a new strategy."

"Some commuter airlines are looking outside their traditional business for new ways of generating revenues. Package-freight services and junkets to ski resorts provide revenue beyond passenger service."

Smith replied, "Although we are using our Beechcraft 1900s in a 300-mile market, there are better planes for the longer routes. In addition, passengers on junkets and vacation runs prefer more luxurious aircraft than Mid-Continent currently owns."

"That is correct," Dr. Golden pointed out. "Some of the new ideas might require larger aircraft, such as the Fairchild Metroliner, British Jetstream, or Brasilia."

Smith looked out the window of his office at a Mid-Continent plane being serviced and replied, "Well, thanks for taking a look at our operation and giving us your opinion. We have a difficult decision to make."

Dr. Golden gathered her papers from off the desk and said, "It was nice meeting you. Good luck on whichever decision you make."

Questions

1. What should the current owners do – sell or keep the business? Justify your answer.

2. Regardless of the decision by the original owners,

    a. Develop a short strategic plan, including objectives and strategies for the future of Mid-Continent.

    b. What markets should Mid-Continent be in? (Be specific. See the list of markets on page 88.)

    c. What should they do about aircraft acquisition? See page 13 in this manual.

    d. What other critical issues does this case present?

Note: For the latest financial statements for this firm, see page 28 in the front of the manual.

QUARTERLY SALES REPORT

Mar-ket #	Round trip Flights Per Day	Round trip Seats Flown Per Day	Round trip Seats Sold Per Day	Load Factor – % of available seats that were sold
1	2	38	22	57.6%
2	3	57	34	59.6%
3	2	38	19	50.0%
4	3	57	36	63.1%
5	3	57	38	66.6%
6	0	0	0	

FLEET STATUS REPORT

A/C Serial No.	Type	Cost	Depreciation	Book Value
1	A	700,000	200,000	500,000
2	A	800,000	250,000	550,000
3	A	1,000,000	350,000	650,000

Note: A Type A aircraft has 19 seats with 4' 6"
headroom and no toilet.

MARKET DATA - LAST QUARTER
(This firm's Geographical Region)

Mkt No.	** This Firm **				** Other Airlines **			
	Round-trip miles	Flights per day	Seats Flown /day	Seats Sold /day	Co No.	Flights per day	Seats Flown /day	Route
1	600	2	38	22	2	2	38	Mini-hub to medium city
2	400	3	57	34	2	3	57	Between 2 cities in their area
3	340	2	38	19	2	2	38	Mini-hub to regional hub
4	360	3	57	36	2	3	57	Mini-hub to medium city
5	400	3	57	38	0	0	0	Mini-hub to medium city
6	420	0	0	0	0	0	0	Mini-Hub to foreign city
7	420	0	0	0	2	3	57	Mini-hub to medium city
8	400	0	0	0	0	0	0	Mini-hub to foreign city
17	600	0	0	0	0	0	0	Their mini-hub to a resort area

In the table above, Total seats per day = # of flights × # of seats in the type aircraft used in that market, e.g., market 1: 2 × 19 = 38. Thus, the airline flew 38 seats per day in market 1 and sold 22 seats for a load factor of 57.8%.

On the following page the itinerary for each of the three aircraft is shown.

QUARTERLY SALES REPORT

Mar-ket #	Round trip Flights Per Day	Round trip Seats Flown Per Day	Round trip Seats Sold Per Day	Load Factor (% of seats that were avail-able which were sold)
1	2	38	22	57.8.6%
2	3	57	34	59.6%
3	2	38	19	50.0%
4	3	57	36	63.1%
5	3	57	38	66.6%
6	0	0	0	

FLEET STATUS REPORT

A/C Serial No.	Type	Cost	Depreciation	Book Value
1	A	700,000	200,000	500,000
2	A	800,000	250,000	550,000
3	A	1,000,000	350,000	650,000

Note: A Type A aircraft has 19 seats with 4'6" headroom and no toilet.

MARKET DATA - LAST QUARTER
(This firm's Geographical Region)

Mkt No.	** This Firm ** Round-trip miles	Flights per day	Seats Flown /day	Seats Sold /day	** Other Airlines ** Co No.	Flights per day	Seats Flown /day	Route
1	600	2	38	22	2	2	38	Mini-hub to medium city
2	400	3	57	34	2	3	57	Between 2 cities in their area
3	340	2	38	19	2	2	38	Mini-hub to regional hub
4	360	3	57	36	2	3	57	Mini-hub to medium city
5	400	3	57	38	0	0	0	Mini-hub to medium city
6	420	0	0	0	0	0	0	Mini-Hub to foreign city
7	400	0	0	0	2	3	57	Mini-hub to medium city
8	400	0	0	0	0			Mini-hub to foreign city
17	600	0	0	0	0			Their mini-hub to a resort area

In the table above, Total seats per day = # of flights x # of seats in the type aircraft used in that market, e.g., market 1: 2 x 19 = 38. Thus, the airline flew 38 seats per day in market 1 and sold 22 seats for a load factor of 57.8%.

TABLE 12: MARKETS SERVED
AIRCRAFT NO. 1 ITINERARY

	Mileage
Flight #1	600
Flight #2	400
Flight #3	400
Flight #4	360
Total Miles Flown	1,760

SECTION 8
DECISION AND ANALYSIS FORMS

This section contains various forms and worksheets to aid your team in making better decisions and to keep abreast of your performance in relation to the industry averages. Decision forms for recording your decisions each period are also included. There are two types of Market Profitability Analysis attached. Some preferred one over the other in our alpha test of the 4th edition, so we are including both versions.

Decision Diary   Industry ___ Co #____

Enter decisions each quarter so there is a master list of decisions retained.

Quarter #	1	2	3	4	5	6	7	8	9	10	11	12
Fare												
Cabin Serv.												
Promotion												
Advertise												
Salesper												
Emp Comp												
% Wages												
Qual/Tng												
Maint												
Fuel												
Cargo $												
SocPerf $												
Stock												
S-T Loan												
L-T Loan												
Dividends												
CD												
#Acquired												
Type												
Lease/Purc												
#Acquired												
Type												
Lease/Purc												
Disposed												
Disposed												
Disposed												
Mkt Res												
Incident												

Market Profitability Analysis: Type 1   **Form 1**

Quarter #____ Industry_____ Co #_____ Prepared By _____

Daily Available Seat Miles (DASM)

Multiply No. of <u>available</u> seats flown   _____

By miles per round trip flown (see Table 12)   × _____ = _____ (a)

Market Roundtrip Revenue (MRR)

Multiply fare per mile   _____

By miles per round trip flown (see Table 12)   × _____ = _____ (b)

  (MRR is the daily revenue in a given market)

When completed, transfer all (a) & (b) values to all lines labeled (a) & (b) below

---

Daily Market Revenue in Market #____

    Multiply No. of seats sold per day in this market (from your quarterly report) _____

    By market round trip revenue (b) × $_____ (b) = _____ (1) = Daily Market Revenue

Total Market Operating Cost in Market # ____

    Multiply cost per available seat mile (from quarterly report) ._____

    By daily available seat miles (a) × _____ (a) = _____ (2) = Market Operating Cost

Breakeven Number of Passengers (the number of passengers needed to pay costs but no profits)
Divide market operating cost (2) $_____

By total revenue (b) $_____   = _____   **(This is the number of passengers in a**

day that is needed to breakeven in this market)

Compare this number with the actual seats sold in that market to ascertain if the market is earning

a profit (from the quarterly report): _____

TABLE 12
Roundtrip Miles Per Market

Number of Miles	Market Numbers
600	1, 9, 21, 30,38, 47, 17, 20, 29, 44
400	2, 10, 22, 31, 39, 48
340	3, 11, 23, 32, 40, 49
360	4, 12, 24, 33, 41, 50
420	5, 13, 25, 34, 42, 51, 7, 15, 18, 27, 36, 45
420	6, 14, 26, 35, 43, 52, 8, 16, 19, 28, 37, 46
600	17, 20, 29, 44

Market Profitability Analysis: Type 2 Market #_____ **Form 2**

Prepared by_____ Team #_____ Industry #_____

Revenues for this Market
    # seats sold daily   _____
    times fare per mile   × 0._____
    times # roundtrip miles in this mkt   × _____
    = Daily Revenue this Market $ _____(1)

Direct Costs
    Total quarterly cost of flight operations + fuel + maintenance
    + passenger service + cabin service $ _____
    divided by total quarterly available seat miles _____ = $ 0.___(2)
    times # avail daily seats provided in this mkt by our firm × (_____) = _____
    times the # of roundtrip miles in this market   × _____
    = Daily Direct Costs in this Market $ _____(3)

Contribution Margin of this Market = Revenues (1)− Direct costs(3) = $_____

OPERATING STATISTICS:

Available seat miles (ASMs) per day
    # avail seats flown daily this market _____
    times miles per round trip   × _____ = _____(4)

Revenue passenger miles (RPMs) per day
    # seats sold/day(_____) × mi. per round trip flight _____ = _____(5)

Yield per available seat mile (in cents)
    Revenues this market from (1) above $_____
    divided by ASMs (4)   ÷ _____ = 0._____

Load factor
    Revenue passenger miles (5)   _____
    divided by ASMs (4)   ÷ _____ = _____%

Breakeven # of passengers (based on direct costs)
    Daily direct costs in this market (3) $_____
    divided by fare per mile   ÷ ._____
    times miles per round trip × _____   = _____ (6)

Breakeven load (as a % per day)
    Breakeven # passengers (6)   _____
    divided by seats flown daily   ÷ _____ = _____

Total operating costs on this route
    Cost per available seat mile (from quarterly report) 0._____
    times daily ASMs this route × _____ = $_____ (7)

Breakeven # passengers (based on total costs) per day
    Fare per mile ._____ times miles per round trip × _____ = _____ (8)
    Daily total costs in this market (7) $_____ ÷ (8)_____ = _____

Note: This is a relatively simple calculation and does not take into account the present value of money nor future income streams. It assumes a 12-year loan. A spreadsheet program (constructed by you) could give a more explicit comparison. One benefit of purchasing is that you are building assets on the balance sheet. However, this also requires obtaining extra capital to pay the principal each quarter. The repayment of principal has no effect on profit and loss but does require additional capital acquisition. On the other hand, leasing is a straightforward approach to acquisition.

AIRCRAFT LEASE/BUY CALCULATIONS: Part 1						
A/C TYPE	1 Quarterly Lease Cost (000)	2 Annual Lease Cost Col 1 x 4 (000)	3 Purchase Price $million	4 Annual Interest Cost Col 3 x .09 (000)	5 Annual Depreciation Col 3 x .08 (000)	6 Total Interest & Depreciation (000)
A	80	320	2.0	180	160	340
B	82	328	2.2	198	176	374
C	132	528	3.1	279	248	527
D	144	576	3.4	306	272	578
E	184	736	4.3	387	344	731
F	185	740	4.4	396	352	748
G	240	960	5.8	522	464	986

AIRCRAFT LEASE/BUY CALCULATIONS: Part 2					
A/C Type	8 After-Tax Annual Lease Cost Col 2 × .06 (000)	9 After-Tax Interest + Depreciation Cost Col 9 × .06 (000)	10 Lowest First-Year Difference: L = Lease B = Buy (000)	11 Asset Base being built each year if purchasing aircraft	12 You need to calculate additional cash flow required if purchasing
A	192	204	L By 12	160	
B	196	224	L by 28	176	
C	317	316	equal	248	
D	442	346	L by 96	272	
E	442	438	L by 4	344	
F	444	448	L by 4	352	
G	576	591	L by 15	464	

FINANCIAL RATIO ANALYSIS   **Form 4-a**

Prepared By _____   Industry ___ Co #____

In order for this information to be meaningful, it should be compared to the ratios the previous quarter and against the industry averages. You should then indicate which of the ratios are not As good as industry averages and state why there is a variance.

LIQUIDITY MEASURES: These indicators show the availability   **Enter**
of cash to meet current expenses.   **Industry**
                                                                       Ratios
Current Ratio: **Below**

$\underline{\text{Cash} + \text{Short-term investment} + \text{Accounts receivable}}$ = _____ = _____   _____
Accounts Payable + Short-term loans

Net Working Capital:

Total current assets − Total current liabilities = _____ − _____ = _____   _____

EFFICIENCY MEASURES: These indicators show the efficient use of assets of the company.

Asset Turnover:

$\underline{\text{Gross Revenue}}$ = _____ = _____   _____
Total Assets

Daily Seat Productivity:

$\underline{\text{Total Quarterly Passengers divided by 80}}$ = _____   _____
Total Seats

LEVERAGE MEASURES: These indicators show the portion of the financing of the company that can be claimed by contract in the event of bankruptcy. They also show the level of fixed expense that cannot be reduced.

Debt-to-Total Assets:

$\underline{\text{Total Liabilities}}$ = _____ = _____   _____
Total Assets

Debt to Equity:

$\underline{\text{Short-term} + \text{long-term debt}}$ = _____ = _____   _____
Common Stock + Ret. Earnings

-over-

**PROFITABILITY MEASURES: These are indicators of the
profitability of the company to the claim holders
(banks, lessors, stockholders).**

Enter
Industry
Ratios
Below

Gross Margin:

$$\frac{\text{Gross Revenue} - \text{Flt Cost} - \text{Fuel} - \text{Maint} - \text{Pass Serv} - \text{Commissions} - \text{Refunds}}{\text{Gross Revenue}} =$$

_____ = _____   _____

Return on Assets:

$$\frac{\text{Profit before tax} + \text{interest expense}}{\text{Total Assets}} = \text{_____} = \text{_____}$$ _____

Return on Investment:

$$\frac{\text{Net Profit}}{\text{Total Assets}} = \text{_____} = \text{_____}$$ _____

Return on Equity:

$$\frac{\text{Net Profit}}{\text{Total Equity}} = \text{_____} = \text{_____}$$ _____

Return on Sales:

$$\frac{\text{Profit after Taxes}}{\text{Gross Revenues}} = \text{_____} = \text{_____}$$ _____

100

Aircraft Scheduling Worksheet   Form 5

Aircraft Number	Mkt # / miles	Mkt # / miles	Mkt # / miles	Mkt # / miles	Mkt # / miles	Total Miles this Aircraft
1	/	/	/	/	/	
2	/	/	/	/	/	
3	/	/	/	/	/	
4	/	/	/	/	/	
5	/	/	/	/	/	
6	/	/	/	/	/	
7	/	/	/	/	/	
8	/	/	/	/	/	
9	/	/	/	/	/	
10	/	/	/	/	/	
11	/	/	/	/	/	
12	/	/	/	/	/	
13	/	/	/	/	/	
14	/	/	/	/	/	
15	/	/	/	/	/	

Objective: Total miles each aircraft should be as close to 1,800 miles as possible. Some aircraft may be a few miles over as long as other aircraft are a few miles short. Use the calculation below to ascertain the total miles per day you may fly.

Number of Aircraft in your fleet _____ times 1,800 miles per day = _____ maximum miles.

Co #___ Ind___ Qtr#___   **AIRLINE DECISION FORM**   Co Name_____

1. **FARE (per seat mile flown) Groups: 28-31, 35-40, 48-51**   Enter in cents (no decimal) _____

2. **CABIN SERVICE**   (Enter 0, 1, 2, or 3) _____
    Key: 0 = No in-flight service
          1 = Free Soft Drinks and Snacks
          2 = Free soft drinks, snacks, and a sandwich during mealtimes
          3 = Free drinks, hors d'oeuvres, meals

3. **PROMOTION BUDGET**   (Enter in $ with no comma) $_____

4. **ADVERTISING BUDGET**   (Enter in $ with no comma) $_____

5. **NUMBER OF NEW SALESPERSONS HIRED <u>THIS QUARTER</u> (max 4 per quarter)**   _____

6. **EMPLOYEE COMPENSATION POLICY**   Entry Key: _____
    Key: 0 = Pay minimum allowable by law or minimum prevailing wage
          1 = Managers and pilots receive ____% above minimum prevailing wage
          2 = Pay ____% above prevailing wage to pilots and professionals only.
          3 = Pay ____% above prevailing wage to all employees, including pilots and professionals
          4 = Pay ____% above prevailing wage to pilots and professionals + stock-bonus
          5 = Pay ____% above prevailing wage to all employees + stock-bonus (includes pilots and professionals)
          6 = Pay ____% above prevailing wage to pilots and professionals + 20% of profits
          7 = Pay ____% above minimum + 20% profits to all employees

7. **Enter % wage increase (if applicable)**   (no decimal) _____%

8. **QUALITY PROGRAMS AND TRAINING (Enter in $ with no comma)** $_____

9. **MAINTENANCE LEVEL**   (Enter Level 1, 2, or 3): _____
          Level 1: Legal minimum maintenance
          Level 2: Legal maintenance; additional 20% spare parts; wash every 3 months
          Level 3: Legal maintenance; additional 40% parts; Preventive Maintenance program; wash every month

10. **FUEL CONTRACT for next quarter**   Entry Key: _____
    Key: 0 = All fuel purchased on the spot market
          1 = 50% purchased on open market and 50% on contract
          2 = All fuel purchased on contract

11. **CARGO MARKETING BUDGET (Minimum $10,000)**   (Enter in $ no comma) $_____

12. **CORPORATE SOCIAL PERFORMANCE BUDGET**   (Enter in $ no comma) $_____

13. **STOCK SOLD: In dollars, <u>not shares</u>**   (Enter in $ no comma) $_____

14. **SHORT-TERM LOAN (use a minus sign to make a loan payment; Enter in $ no comma)** $_____

15. **LONG-TERM LOAN (use minus sign to make an <u>extra</u> loan payment; Enter $ no comma)** $_____

16. **DIVIDENDS DECLARED (total dollars to be paid; lack of profits will void)** $_____

17. **NINETY-TWO DAY CERTIFICATE OF DEPOSIT PURCHASED   (Enter in $ no comma)** $_____

VERIFICATION TOTAL FOR ITEMS 1 to 17   [_____]

Notes: 1. Verification Total is for computer entry verification only. Include items 1 to 17. Subtract negative numbers. (2) All items except #5 to be entered each quarter even if there is no change. (3) Loan payment in addition to automatic payment.

Co #___ Ind___ Qtr#___   **AIRLINE DECISION FORM**

FIRST ACQUISITION TRANSACTION:
18. Number of Aircraft (0 - 4)   _____   (See page 12)
19. Type of Aircraft (A - G)   _____
20. Lease (1) or Purchase (2)   _____

SECOND ACQUISITION TRANSACTION:
21. Number of Aircraft (0 - 4)   _____
22. Type of Aircraft (A - G)   _____
23. Lease (1) or Purchase (2)_   _____

24. Serial Number of First Aircraft Disposal   _____   (Use this space first if disposing. See page 14)
25. Serial Number of Second Aircraft Disposal   _____
26. Serial Number of Third Aircraft Disposal   _____

27. Total Cost of Market Research Studies $_____   ($0 to 31000. See pg 14)

28. Incident Response   _____   (You **must** know the incident being used)

VERIFICATION TOTAL FOR ITEMS 18 to 28   [   ]
   NOTE: Verification Total is for computer entry
         verification only. Add all numbers.

29. **CHANGES IN MARKETS SERVED:** Enter only the markets in which you have a change. If changing any items in a currently held market, enter all items even though you may be changing only one item this period. Enter zeros beside a market you wish to abandon. A Fare Sale must be entered each quarter for each market if you wish to continue it.

Market	Round Trip Flights per day	Total Seats (Flights times Seats on all A/C in this market)	Type of Fare Sale (0 - 3)
An Example >> 8	3	3-19 seat A/C=57	1
_____	_____	_____	_____
_____	_____	_____	_____
_____	_____	_____	_____
_____	_____	_____	_____
_____	_____	_____	_____
_____	_____	_____	_____
_____	_____	_____	_____
_____	_____	_____	_____
_____	_____	_____	_____
_____	_____	_____	_____
_____	_____	_____	_____
_____	_____	_____	_____
_____	_____	_____	_____
_____	_____	_____	_____

✔ **The most common error in completing the MARKETS SERVED form is to enter the number of seats on ONE aircraft and not multiply that number time the number of flights.**

MAXIMUM NUMBER OF MARKET CHANGES = 14. See page 14 for additional information.

Co #____ Ind____ Qtr#____ **AIRLINE DECISION FORM** Co Name_____

1. FARE (per seat mile flown) Groups: 28-31, 35-40, 48-51   Enter in cents (no decimal) _____

2. CABIN SERVICE   (Enter 0, 1, 2, or 3) _____
  Key: 0 = No in-flight service
        1 = Free Soft Drinks and Snacks
        2 = Free soft drinks, snacks, and a sandwich during mealtimes
        3 = Free drinks, hors d'oeuvres, meals

3. PROMOTION BUDGET   (Enter in $ with no comma) $_____

4. ADVERTISING BUDGET   (Enter in $ with no comma) $_____

5. NUMBER OF NEW SALESPERSONS HIRED <u>THIS QUARTER</u> (max 4 per quarter)   ____

6. EMPLOYEE COMPENSATION POLICY   Entry Key: _____
  Key: 0 = Pay minimum allowable by law or minimum prevailing wage
        1 = Managers and pilots receive ____% above minimum prevailing wage
        2 = Pay ____% above prevailing wage to pilots and professionals only.
        3 = Pay ____% above prevailing wage to all employees, including pilots and professionals
        4 = Pay ____% above prevailing wage to pilots and professionals + stock-bonus
        5 = Pay ____% above prevailing wage to all employees + stock-bonus (includes pilots and professionals)
        6 = Pay ____% above prevailing wage to pilots and professionals + 20% of profits
        7 = Pay ____% above minimum + 20% profits to all employees

7. Enter % wage increase (if applicable)   (no decimal) _____%

8. QUALITY PROGRAMS AND TRAINING (Enter in $ with no comma) $_____

9. MAINTENANCE LEVEL   (Enter Level 1, 2, or 3): _____
        Level 1: Legal minimum maintenance
        Level 2: Legal maintenance; additional 20% spare parts; wash every 3 months
        Level 3: Legal maintenance; additional 40% parts; Preventive Maintenance program; wash every month

10. FUEL CONTRACT for next quarter   **Entry Key:** _____
  Key: 0 = All fuel purchased on the spot market
       1 = 50% purchased on open market and 50% on contract
       2 = All fuel purchased on contract

11. CARGO MARKETING BUDGET (Minimum $10,000)   (Enter in $ no comma) $_____

12. CORPORATE SOCIAL PERFORMANCE BUDGET   (Enter in $ no comma) $_____

13. STOCK SOLD: In dollars, <u>not shares</u>   (Enter in $ no comma) $_____

14. SHORT-TERM LOAN (use a minus sign to make a loan payment; Enter in $ no comma) $_____

15. LONG-TERM LOAN (use minus sign to make an <u>extra</u> loan payment; Enter $ no comma) $_____

16. DIVIDENDS DECLARED (total dollars to be paid; lack of profits will void) $_____

17. NINETY-TWO DAY CERTIFICATE OF DEPOSIT PURCHASED   (Enter in $ no comma)$_____

VERIFICATION TOTAL FOR ITEMS 1 to 17   [   ]

Notes: 1. Verification Total is for computer entry verification only. Include items 1 to 17. Subtract negative numbers. (2) All items except #5 to be entered each quarter even if there is no change. (3) Loan payment in addition to automatic payment.

Co #___ Ind___ Qtr#___   **AIRLINE DECISION FORM**

FIRST ACQUISITION TRANSACTION:
18. Number of Aircraft (0 - 4)   _____   (See page 12)
19. Type of Aircraft (A - G)   _____
20. Lease (1) or Purchase (2)   _____

SECOND ACQUISITION TRANSACTION:
21. Number of Aircraft (0 - 4)   _____
22. Type of Aircraft (A - G)   _____
23. Lease (1) or Purchase (2)_   _____

24. Serial Number of First Aircraft Disposal   _____   (Use this space first if disposing. See page 14)
25. Serial Number of Second Aircraft Disposal   _____
26. Serial Number of Third Aircraft Disposal   _____

27. Total Cost of Market Research Studies $_____   ($0 to 31000. See pg 14)

28. Incident Response   _____   (You **must** know the incident being used)

VERIFICATION TOTAL FOR ITEMS 18 to 28   [   ]
    NOTE: Verification Total is for computer entry
    verification only. Add all numbers.

29. CHANGES IN MARKETS SERVED: <u>Enter only the markets in which you have a change</u>. If changing any items in a currently held market, enter all items even though you may be changing only one item this period. Enter zeros beside a market you wish to abandon. A Fare Sale must be entered <u>each quarter</u> for each market if you wish to continue it.

Market	Round Trip Flights per day	Total Seats (Flights times Seats on all A/C in this market)	Type of Fare Sale (0 - 3)
An Example >> 8	3	3-19 seat A/C=57	1
_____	_____	_____	_____
_____	_____	_____	_____
_____	_____	_____	_____
_____	_____	_____	_____
_____	_____	_____	_____
_____	_____	_____	_____
_____	_____	_____	_____
_____	_____	_____	_____
_____	_____	_____	_____
_____	_____	_____	_____
_____	_____	_____	_____
_____	_____	_____	_____
_____	_____	_____	_____
_____	_____	_____	_____

✔ **The most common error in completing the MARKETS SERVED form is to enter the number of seats on ONE aircraft and not multiply that number time the number of flights.**

MAXIMUM NUMBER OF MARKET CHANGES = 14. See page 14 for additional information.

Co #___ Ind___ Qtr#___   AIRLINE DECISION FORM   Co Name_____

1. FARE (per seat mile flown) Groups: 28-31, 35-40, 48-51   Enter in cents (no decimal) _____

2. CABIN SERVICE   (Enter 0, 1, 2, or 3) _____
   Key: 0 = No in-flight service
           1 = Free Soft Drinks and Snacks
           2 = Free soft drinks, snacks, and a sandwich during mealtimes
           3 = Free drinks, hors d'oeuvres, meals

3. PROMOTION BUDGET   (Enter in $ with no comma) $_____

4. ADVERTISING BUDGET   (Enter in $ with no comma) $_____

5. NUMBER OF NEW SALESPERSONS HIRED <u>THIS QUARTER</u> (max 4 per quarter)   ____

6. EMPLOYEE COMPENSATION POLICY   Entry Key: _____
   Key: 0 = Pay minimum allowable by law or minimum prevailing wage
           1 = Managers and pilots receive _____% above minimum prevailing wage
           2 = Pay _____% above prevailing wage to pilots and professionals only.
           3 = Pay _____% above prevailing wage to all employees, including pilots and professionals
           4 = Pay _____% above prevailing wage to pilots and professionals + stock-bonus
           5 = Pay _____% above prevailing wage to all employees + stock-bonus (includes pilots and professionals)
           6 = Pay _____% above prevailing wage to pilots and professionals + 20% of profits
           7 = Pay _____% above minimum + 20% profits to all employees

7. Enter % wage increase (if applicable)   (no decimal) _____%

8. QUALITY PROGRAMS AND TRAINING (Enter in $ with no comma) $_____

9. MAINTENANCE LEVEL   (Enter Level 1, 2, or 3): _____
    Level 1: Legal minimum maintenance
    Level 2: Legal maintenance; additional 20% spare parts; wash every 3 months
    Level 3: Legal maintenance; additional 40% parts; Preventive Maintenance program; wash every month

10. FUEL CONTRACT for next quarter   **Entry Key:** _____
   Key: 0 = All fuel purchased on the spot market
          1 = 50% purchased on open market and 50% on contract
          2 = All fuel purchased on contract

11. CARGO MARKETING BUDGET (Minimum $10,000)   (Enter in $ no comma) $_____

12. CORPORATE SOCIAL PERFORMANCE BUDGET   (Enter in $ no comma) $_____

13. STOCK SOLD: In dollars, <u>not shares</u>   (Enter in $ no comma) $_____

14. SHORT-TERM LOAN (use a minus sign to make a loan payment; Enter in $ no comma) $_____

15. LONG-TERM LOAN (use minus sign to make an <u>extra</u> loan payment; Enter $ no comma) $_____

16. DIVIDENDS DECLARED (total dollars to be paid; lack of profits will void) $_____

17. NINETY-TWO DAY CERTIFICATE OF DEPOSIT PURCHASED (Enter in $ no comma)$_____

          VERIFICATION TOTAL FOR ITEMS 1 to 17   [_____]

Notes: 1. Verification Total is for computer entry verification only. Include items 1 to 17. Subtract negative numbers. (2) All
items except #5 to be entered each quarter even if there is no change. (3) Loan payment in addition to automatic payment.

Co #___ Ind___ Qtr#___   AIRLINE DECISION FORM

FIRST ACQUISITION TRANSACTION:
18. Number of Aircraft (0 - 4)   _____   (See page 12)
19. Type of Aircraft (A - G)   _____
20. Lease (1) or Purchase (2)   _____

SECOND ACQUISITION TRANSACTION:
21. Number of Aircraft (0 - 4)   _____
22. Type of Aircraft (A - G)   _____
23. Lease (1) or Purchase (2)_   _____

24. Serial Number of First Aircraft Disposal   _____   (Use this space first if disposing. See page 14)
25. Serial Number of Second Aircraft Disposal   _____
26. Serial Number of Third Aircraft Disposal   _____

27. Total Cost of Market Research Studies $_____   ($0 to 31000. See pg 14)

28. Incident Response   _____   (You **must** know the incident being used)

VERIFICATION TOTAL FOR ITEMS 18 to 28
> NOTE: Verification Total is for computer entry
> verification only. Add all numbers.

29. CHANGES IN MARKETS SERVED: Enter only the markets in which you have a change. If changing any items in a currently held market, enter all items even though you may be changing only one item this period. Enter zeros beside a market you wish to abandon. A Fare Sale must be entered **each quarter** for each market if you wish to continue it.

	Market	Round Trip Flights per day	Total Seats (Flights times Seats on all A/C in this market)	Type of Fare Sale (0 - 3)
An Example >>	8	3	3-19 seat A/C=57	1
	____	____	_____	_____
	____	____	_____	_____
	____	____	_____	_____
	____	____	_____	_____
	____	____	_____	_____
	____	____	_____	_____
	____	____	_____	_____
	____	____	_____	_____
	____	____	_____	_____
	____	____	_____	_____
	____	____	_____	_____
	____	____	_____	_____
	____	____	_____	_____
	____	____	_____	_____

✔ **The most common error in completing the MARKETS SERVED form is to enter the number of seats on ONE aircraft and not multiply that number time the number of flights.**

MAXIMUM NUMBER OF MARKET CHANGES = 14. See page 14 for additional information.

Co #___ Ind___ Qtr#___ AIRLINE DECISION FORM   Co Name_____

1. FARE (per seat mile flown) Groups: 28-31, 35-40, 48-51   Enter in cents (no decimal) _____

2. CABIN SERVICE   (Enter 0, 1, 2, or 3) _____
    Key: 0 = No in-flight service
          1 = Free Soft Drinks and Snacks
          2 = Free soft drinks, snacks, and a sandwich during mealtimes
          3 = Free drinks, hors d'oeuvres, meals

3. PROMOTION BUDGET   (Enter in $ with no comma) $_____

4. ADVERTISING BUDGET   (Enter in $ with no comma) $_____

5. NUMBER OF NEW SALESPERSONS HIRED <u>THIS QUARTER</u> (max 4 per quarter)   ____

6. EMPLOYEE COMPENSATION POLICY   Entry Key: _____
    Key: 0 = Pay minimum allowable by law or minimum prevailing wage
          1 = Managers and pilots receive _____% above minimum prevailing wage
          2 = Pay _____% above prevailing wage to pilots and professionals only.
          3 = Pay _____% above prevailing wage to all employees, including pilots and professionals
          4 = Pay _____% above prevailing wage to pilots and professionals + stock-bonus
          5 = Pay _____% above prevailing wage to all employees + stock-bonus (includes pilots and professionals)
          6 = Pay _____% above prevailing wage to pilots and professionals + 20% of profits
          7 = Pay _____% above minimum + 20% profits to all employees

7. Enter % wage increase (if applicable)   (no decimal) _____%

8. QUALITY PROGRAMS AND TRAINING (Enter in $ with no comma) $_____

9. MAINTENANCE LEVEL   (Enter Level 1, 2, or 3): _____
        Level 1: Legal minimum maintenance
        Level 2: Legal maintenance; additional 20% spare parts; wash every 3 months
        Level 3: Legal maintenance; additional 40% parts; Preventive Maintenance program; wash every month

10. FUEL CONTRACT for next quarter   Entry Key: _____
    Key: 0 = All fuel purchased on the spot market
          1 = 50% purchased on open market and 50% on contract
          2 = All fuel purchased on contract

11. CARGO MARKETING BUDGET (Minimum $10,000)   (Enter in $ no comma) $_____

12. CORPORATE SOCIAL PERFORMANCE BUDGET   (Enter in $ no comma) $_____

13. STOCK SOLD: In dollars, <u>not shares</u>   (Enter in $ no comma) $_____

14. SHORT-TERM LOAN (use a minus sign to make a loan payment; Enter in $ no comma) $_____

15. LONG-TERM LOAN (use minus sign to make an <u>extra</u> loan payment; Enter $ no comma) $_____

16. DIVIDENDS DECLARED (total dollars to be paid; lack of profits will void) $_____

17. NINETY-TWO DAY CERTIFICATE OF DEPOSIT PURCHASED   (Enter in $ no comma)$_____

                    VERIFICATION TOTAL FOR ITEMS 1 to 17   [_____]

Notes: 1. Verification Total is for computer entry verification only. Include items 1 to 17. Subtract negative numbers. (2) All items except #5 to be entered each quarter even if there is no change. (3) Loan payment in addition to automatic payment.

Co #___ Ind___ Qtr#___ **AIRLINE DECISION FORM**

FIRST ACQUISITION TRANSACTION:
18. Number of Aircraft (0 - 4)   _____ (See page 12)
19. Type of Aircraft (A - G)   _____
20. Lease (1) or Purchase (2)   _____

SECOND ACQUISITION TRANSACTION:
21. Number of Aircraft (0 - 4)   _____
22. Type of Aircraft (A - G)   _____
23. Lease (1) or Purchase (2)_   _____

24. Serial Number of First Aircraft Disposal   _____ (Use this space first if disposing. See page 14)
25. Serial Number of Second Aircraft Disposal   _____
26. Serial Number of Third Aircraft Disposal   _____

27. Total Cost of Market Research Studies $_____ ($0 to 31000. See pg 14)

28. Incident Response   _____ (You <u>must</u> know the incident being used)

VERIFICATION TOTAL FOR ITEMS 18 to 28   ☐
    NOTE: Verification Total is for computer entry
        verification only. Add all numbers.

29. **CHANGES IN MARKETS SERVED:** <u>Enter only the markets in which you have a change</u>. If changing any items in a currently held market, enter all items even though you may be changing only one item this period. Enter zeros beside a market you wish to abandon. A Fare Sale must be entered <u>each quarter</u> for each market if you wish to continue it.

	Market	Round Trip Flights per day	Total Seats (Flights times Seats on all A/C in this market)	Type of Fare Sale (0 - 3)
An Example >>	8	3	3-19 seat A/C=57	1
	____	____	_____	____
	____	____	_____	____
	____	____	_____	____
	____	____	_____	____
	____	____	_____	____
	____	____	_____	____
	____	____	_____	____
	____	____	_____	____
	____	____	_____	____
	____	____	_____	____
	____	____	_____	____
	____	____	_____	____
	____	____	_____	____
	____	____	_____	____

✔ **The most common error in completing the MARKETS SERVED form is to enter the number of seats on ONE aircraft and not multiply that number time the number of flights.**

MAXIMUM NUMBER OF MARKET CHANGES = 14. See page 14 for additional information.

Co #___ Ind___ Qtr#___ **AIRLINE DECISION FORM** Co Name_____ .

1. **FARE** (per seat mile flown) Groups: 28-31, 35-40, 48-51   Enter in cents (no decimal) _____

2. **CABIN SERVICE**   (Enter 0, 1, 2, or 3) _____
   Key: 0 = No in-flight service
         1 = Free Soft Drinks and Snacks
         2 = Free soft drinks, snacks, and a sandwich during mealtimes
         3 = Free drinks, hors d'oeuvres, meals

3. **PROMOTION BUDGET**   (Enter in $ with no comma) $_____

4. **ADVERTISING BUDGET**   (Enter in $ with no comma) $_____

5. **NUMBER OF NEW SALESPERSONS HIRED THIS QUARTER** (max 4 per quarter)   ____

6. **EMPLOYEE COMPENSATION POLICY**   Entry Key: _____
   Key: 0 = Pay minimum allowable by law or minimum prevailing wage
         1 = Managers and pilots receive ____% above minimum prevailing wage
         2 = Pay ____% above prevailing wage to pilots and professionals only.
         3 = Pay ____% above prevailing wage to all employees, including pilots and professionals
         4 = Pay ____% above prevailing wage to pilots and professionals + stock-bonus
         5 = Pay ____% above prevailing wage to all employees + stock-bonus (includes pilots and professionals)
         6 = Pay ____% above prevailing wage to pilots and professionals + 20% of profits
         7 = Pay ____% above minimum + 20% profits to all employees

7. Enter % wage increase (if applicable)   (no decimal) _____%

8. **QUALITY PROGRAMS AND TRAINING** (Enter in $ with no comma) $_____

9. **MAINTENANCE LEVEL**   (Enter Level 1, 2, or 3): _____
   Level 1: Legal minimum maintenance
   Level 2: Legal maintenance; additional 20% spare parts; wash every 3 months
   Level 3: Legal maintenance; additional 40% parts; Preventive Maintenance program; wash every month

10. **FUEL CONTRACT for next quarter**   **Entry Key:** _____
    Key: 0 = All fuel purchased on the spot market
          1 = 50% purchased on open market and 50% on contract
          2 = All fuel purchased on contract

11. **CARGO MARKETING BUDGET** (Minimum $10,000)   (Enter in $ no comma) $_____

12. **CORPORATE SOCIAL PERFORMANCE BUDGET**   (Enter in $ no comma) $_____

13. **STOCK SOLD:** In dollars, not shares   (Enter in $ no comma) $_____

14. **SHORT-TERM LOAN** (use a minus sign to make a loan payment; Enter in $ no comma) $_____

15. **LONG-TERM LOAN** (use minus sign to make an extra loan payment; Enter $ no comma) $_____

16. **DIVIDENDS DECLARED** (total dollars to be paid; lack of profits will void) $_____

17. **NINETY-TWO DAY CERTIFICATE OF DEPOSIT PURCHASED** (Enter in $ no comma)$_____

VERIFICATION TOTAL FOR ITEMS 1 to 17   [_____]

Notes: 1. Verification Total is for computer entry verification only. Include items 1 to 17. Subtract negative numbers. (2) All items except #5 to be entered each quarter even if there is no change. (3) Loan payment in addition to automatic payment.

Co #___ Ind___ Qtr#___   **AIRLINE DECISION FORM**

FIRST ACQUISITION TRANSACTION:
18. **Number of Aircraft (0 - 4)**   _____ (See page 12)
19. **Type of Aircraft (A - G)**   _____
20. **Lease (1) or Purchase (2)**   _____

SECOND ACQUISITION TRANSACTION:
21. **Number of Aircraft (0 - 4)**   _____
22. **Type of Aircraft (A - G)**   _____
23. **Lease (1) or Purchase (2)_**   _____

24. **Serial Number of First Aircraft Disposal**   _____ (Use this space first if disposing. See page 14)
25. **Serial Number of Second Aircraft Disposal**   _____
26. **Serial Number of Third Aircraft Disposal**   _____

27. **Total Cost of Market Research Studies** $_____ ($0 to 31000. See pg 14)

28. **Incident Response**   _____ (You <u>must</u> know the incident being used)

VERIFICATION TOTAL FOR ITEMS 18 to 28   [   ]
   NOTE: Verification Total is for computer entry
   verification only. Add all numbers.

29. **CHANGES IN MARKETS SERVED:** <u>Enter only the markets in which you have a change.</u> If changing any items in a currently held market, enter all items even though you may be changing only one item this period. Enter zeros beside a market you wish to abandon. A Fare Sale must be entered <u>each quarter</u> for each market if you wish to continue it.

	Market	Round Trip Flights per day	Total Seats (Flights times Seats on all A/C in this market)	Type of Fare Sale (0 - 3)
An Example >>	8	3	3-19 seat A/C=57	1
	_____	_____	_____	_____
	_____	_____	_____	_____
	_____	_____	_____	_____
	_____	_____	_____	_____
	_____	_____	_____	_____
	_____	_____	_____	_____
	_____	_____	_____	_____
	_____	_____	_____	_____
	_____	_____	_____	_____
	_____	_____	_____	_____
	_____	_____	_____	_____
	_____	_____	_____	_____
	_____	_____	_____	_____
	_____	_____	_____	_____

✔ **The most common error in completing the MARKETS SERVED form is to enter the number of seats on ONE aircraft and not multiply that number time the number of flights.**

MAXIMUM NUMBER OF MARKET CHANGES = 14. See page 14 for additional information.

Co #___ Ind___ Qtr#___ **AIRLINE DECISION FORM** Co Name_____

1. FARE (per seat mile flown) Groups: 28-31, 35-40, 48-51   Enter in cents (no decimal) _____

2. CABIN SERVICE   (Enter 0, 1, 2, or 3) _____
    Key: 0 = No in-flight service
             1 = Free Soft Drinks and Snacks
             2 = Free soft drinks, snacks, and a sandwich during mealtimes
             3 = Free drinks, hors d'oeuvres, meals

3. PROMOTION BUDGET   (Enter in $ with no comma) $_____

4. ADVERTISING BUDGET   (Enter in $ with no comma) $_____

5. NUMBER OF NEW SALESPERSONS HIRED <u>THIS QUARTER</u> (max 4 per quarter)   ____

6. EMPLOYEE COMPENSATION POLICY   Entry Key: _____
    Key: 0 = Pay minimum allowable by law or minimum prevailing wage
             1 = Managers and pilots receive ____% above minimum prevailing wage
             2 = Pay ____% above prevailing wage to pilots and professionals only.
             3 = Pay ____% above prevailing wage to all employees, including pilots and professionals
             4 = Pay ____% above prevailing wage to pilots and professionals + stock-bonus
             5 = Pay ____% above prevailing wage to all employees + stock-bonus (includes pilots and professionals)
             6 = Pay ____% above prevailing wage to pilots and professionals + 20% of profits
             7 = Pay ____% above minimum + 20% profits to all employees

7. Enter % wage increase (if applicable)   (no decimal) _____%

8. QUALITY PROGRAMS AND TRAINING (Enter in $ with no comma) $_____

9. MAINTENANCE LEVEL   (Enter Level 1, 2, or 3): _____
        Level 1: Legal minimum maintenance
        Level 2: Legal maintenance; additional 20% spare parts; wash every 3 months
        Level 3: Legal maintenance; additional 40% parts; Preventive Maintenance program; wash every month

10. FUEL CONTRACT for next quarter   Entry Key: _____
    Key: 0 = All fuel purchased on the spot market
             1 = 50% purchased on open market and 50% on contract
             2 = All fuel purchased on contract

11. CARGO MARKETING BUDGET (Minimum $10,000)   (Enter in $ no comma) $_____

12. CORPORATE SOCIAL PERFORMANCE BUDGET   (Enter in $ no comma) $_____

13. STOCK SOLD: In dollars, <u>not shares</u>   (Enter in $ no comma) $_____

14. SHORT-TERM LOAN (use a minus sign to make a loan payment; Enter in $ no comma) $_____

15. LONG-TERM LOAN (use minus sign to make an <u>extra</u> loan payment; Enter $ no comma) $_____

16. DIVIDENDS DECLARED (total dollars to be paid; lack of profits will void) $_____

17. NINETY-TWO DAY CERTIFICATE OF DEPOSIT PURCHASED (Enter in $ no comma)$_____

                  VERIFICATION TOTAL FOR ITEMS 1 to 17   [   ]

Notes: 1. Verification Total is for computer entry verification only. Include items 1 to 17. Subtract negative numbers. (2) All items except #5 to be entered each quarter even if there is no change. (3) Loan payment in addition to automatic payment.

Co #___ Ind___ Qtr#___ **AIRLINE DECISION FORM**

FIRST ACQUISITION TRANSACTION:
18. Number of Aircraft (0 - 4)   _____ (See page 12)
19. Type of Aircraft (A - G)   _____
20. Lease (1) or Purchase (2)   _____

SECOND ACQUISITION TRANSACTION:
21. Number of Aircraft (0 - 4)   _____
22. Type of Aircraft (A - G)   _____
23. Lease (1) or Purchase (2)_   _____

24. Serial Number of First Aircraft Disposal   _____ (Use this space first if disposing. See page 14)
25. Serial Number of Second Aircraft Disposal   _____
26. Serial Number of Third Aircraft Disposal   _____

27. Total Cost of Market Research Studies $_____ ($0 to 31000. See pg 14)

28. Incident Response   _____ (You <u>must</u> know the incident being used)

VERIFICATION TOTAL FOR ITEMS 18 to 28
    NOTE: Verification Total is for computer entry
          verification only. Add all numbers.

29. CHANGES IN MARKETS SERVED: <u>Enter only the markets in which you have a change.</u> If changing any items in a currently held market, enter all items even though you may be changing only one item this period. Enter zeros beside a market you wish to abandon. A Fare Sale must be entered <u>each quarter</u> for each market if you wish to continue it.

Market	Round Trip Flights per day	Total Seats (Flights times Seats on all A/C in this market)	Type of Fare Sale (0 - 3)
An Example >> 8	3	3-19 seat A/C=57	1
_____	_____	_____	_____
_____	_____	_____	_____
_____	_____	_____	_____
_____	_____	_____	_____
_____	_____	_____	_____
_____	_____	_____	_____
_____	_____	_____	_____
_____	_____	_____	_____
_____	_____	_____	_____
_____	_____	_____	_____
_____	_____	_____	_____
_____	_____	_____	_____
_____	_____	_____	_____
_____	_____	_____	_____

✔ **The most common error in completing the MARKETS SERVED form is to enter the number of seats on ONE aircraft and not multiply that number time the number of flights.**

MAXIMUM NUMBER OF MARKET CHANGES = 14. See page 14 for additional information.
© 2002 Software license requires new student manuals each semester used. Illegal to use otherwise.

Co #___ Ind___ Qtr#___   AIRLINE DECISION FORM   Co Name_____

1. **FARE (per seat mile flown) Groups: 28-31, 35-40, 48-51**   Enter in cents (no decimal) _____

2. **CABIN SERVICE**   (Enter 0, 1, 2, or 3) _____
   Key: 0 = No in-flight service
          1 = Free Soft Drinks and Snacks
          2 = Free soft drinks, snacks, and a sandwich during mealtimes
          3 = Free drinks, hors d'oeuvres, meals

3. **PROMOTION BUDGET**   (Enter in $ with no comma) $_____

4. **ADVERTISING BUDGET**   (Enter in $ with no comma) $_____

5. **NUMBER OF NEW SALESPERSONS HIRED <u>THIS QUARTER</u> (max 4 per quarter)**   ____

6. **EMPLOYEE COMPENSATION POLICY**   Entry Key: _____
   Key: 0 = Pay minimum allowable by law or minimum prevailing wage
          1 = Managers and pilots receive ____% above minimum prevailing wage
          2 = Pay ____% above prevailing wage to pilots and professionals only.
          3 = Pay ____% above prevailing wage to all employees, including pilots and professionals
          4 = Pay ____% above prevailing wage to pilots and professionals + stock-bonus
          5 = Pay ____% above prevailing wage to all employees + stock-bonus (includes pilots and professionals)
          6 = Pay ____% above prevailing wage to pilots and professionals + 20% of profits
          7 = Pay ____% above minimum + 20% profits to all employees

7. **Enter % wage increase (if applicable)**   (no decimal)   _____%

8. **QUALITY PROGRAMS AND TRAINING (Enter in $ with no comma)** $_____

9. **MAINTENANCE LEVEL**   (Enter Level 1, 2, or 3): _____
   Level 1: Legal minimum maintenance
   Level 2: Legal maintenance; additional 20% spare parts; wash every 3 months
   Level 3: Legal maintenance; additional 40% parts; Preventive Maintenance program; wash every month

10. **FUEL CONTRACT for next quarter**   **Entry Key: _____**
    Key: 0 = All fuel purchased on the spot market
         1 = 50% purchased on open market and 50% on contract
         2 = All fuel purchased on contract

11. **CARGO MARKETING BUDGET (Minimum $10,000)**   (Enter in $ no comma) $_____

12. **CORPORATE SOCIAL PERFORMANCE BUDGET**   (Enter in $ no comma) $_____

13. **STOCK SOLD: In dollars, <u>not shares</u>**   (Enter in $ no comma) $_____

14. **SHORT-TERM LOAN (use a minus sign to make a loan payment; Enter in $ no comma)** $_____

15. **LONG-TERM LOAN (use minus sign to make an <u>extra</u> loan payment; Enter $ no comma)** $_____

16. **DIVIDENDS DECLARED (total dollars to be paid; lack of profits will void)** $_____

17. **NINETY-TWO DAY CERTIFICATE OF DEPOSIT PURCHASED**   (Enter in $ no comma)$_____

VERIFICATION TOTAL FOR ITEMS 1 to 17   [_____]

Notes: 1. Verification Total is for computer entry verification only. Include items 1 to 17. Subtract negative numbers. (2) All items except #5 to be entered each quarter even if there is no change. (3) Loan payment in addition to automatic payment.

Co #___ Ind___ Qtr#___ **AIRLINE DECISION FORM**

FIRST ACQUISITION TRANSACTION:
18. Number of Aircraft (0 - 4)   _____ (See page 12)
19. Type of Aircraft (A - G)   _____
20. Lease (1) or Purchase (2)   _____

SECOND ACQUISITION TRANSACTION:
21. Number of Aircraft (0 - 4)   _____
22. Type of Aircraft (A - G)   _____
23. Lease (1) or Purchase (2)_   _____

24. Serial Number of First Aircraft Disposal   _____ (Use this space first if disposing. See page 14)
25. Serial Number of Second Aircraft Disposal   _____
26. Serial Number of Third Aircraft Disposal   _____

27. Total Cost of Market Research Studies $_____ ($0 to 31000. See pg 14)

28. Incident Response   _____ (You **must** know the incident being used)

VERIFICATION TOTAL FOR ITEMS 18 to 28   [   ]
    NOTE: Verification Total is for computer entry
    verification only. Add all numbers.

29. **CHANGES IN MARKETS SERVED:** Enter only the markets in which you have a change. If changing any items in a currently held market, enter all items even though you may be changing only one item this period. Enter zeros beside a market you wish to abandon. A Fare Sale must be entered each quarter for each market if you wish to continue it.

Market	Round Trip Flights per day	Total Seats (Flights times Seats on all A/C in this market)	Type of Fare Sale (0 - 3)
An Example >> 8	3	3-19 seat A/C=57	1
_____	_____	_____	_____
_____	_____	_____	_____
_____	_____	_____	_____
_____	_____	_____	_____
_____	_____	_____	_____
_____	_____	_____	_____
_____	_____	_____	_____
_____	_____	_____	_____
_____	_____	_____	_____
_____	_____	_____	_____
_____	_____	_____	_____
_____	_____	_____	_____
_____	_____	_____	_____
_____	_____	_____	_____

✔ **The most common error in completing the MARKETS SERVED form is to enter the number of seats on ONE aircraft and not multiply that number time the number of flights.**

MAXIMUM NUMBER OF MARKET CHANGES = 14. See page 14 for additional information.

Co #___ Ind___ Qtr#___ **AIRLINE DECISION FORM** Co Name_____

1. **FARE (per seat mile flown) Groups: 28-31, 35-40, 48-51**   Enter in cents (no decimal) _____

2. **CABIN SERVICE**   (Enter 0, 1, 2, or 3) _____
   Key: 0 = No in-flight service
         1 = Free Soft Drinks and Snacks
         2 = Free soft drinks, snacks, and a sandwich during mealtimes
         3 = Free drinks, hors d'oeuvres, meals

3. **PROMOTION BUDGET**   (Enter in $ with no comma) $_____

4. **ADVERTISING BUDGET**   (Enter in $ with no comma) $_____

5. **NUMBER OF NEW SALESPERSONS HIRED** THIS QUARTER (max 4 per quarter)   _____

6. **EMPLOYEE COMPENSATION POLICY**   Entry Key: _____
   Key: 0 = Pay minimum allowable by law or minimum prevailing wage
         1 = Managers and pilots receive ____% above minimum prevailing wage
         2 = Pay ____% above prevailing wage to pilots and professionals only.
         3 = Pay ____% above prevailing wage to all employees, including pilots and professionals
         4 = Pay ____% above prevailing wage to pilots and professionals + stock-bonus
         5 = Pay ____% above prevailing wage to all employees + stock-bonus (includes pilots and professionals)
         6 = Pay ____% above prevailing wage to pilots and professionals + 20% of profits
         7 = Pay ____% above minimum + 20% profits to all employees

7. **Enter % wage increase (if applicable)**   (no decimal) _____%

8. **QUALITY PROGRAMS AND TRAINING (Enter in $ with no comma)** $_____

9. **MAINTENANCE LEVEL**   (Enter Level 1, 2, or 3): _____
      Level 1: Legal minimum maintenance
      Level 2: Legal maintenance; additional 20% spare parts; wash every 3 months
      Level 3: Legal maintenance; additional 40% parts; Preventive Maintenance program; wash every month

10. **FUEL CONTRACT for next quarter**   Entry Key: _____
    Key: 0 = All fuel purchased on the spot market
          1 = 50% purchased on open market and 50% on contract
          2 = All fuel purchased on contract

11. **CARGO MARKETING BUDGET (Minimum $10,000)**   (Enter in $ no comma) $_____

12. **CORPORATE SOCIAL PERFORMANCE BUDGET**   (Enter in $ no comma) $_____

13. **STOCK SOLD: In dollars, not shares**   (Enter in $ no comma) $_____

14. **SHORT-TERM LOAN (use a minus sign to make a loan payment; Enter in $ no comma)** $_____

15. **LONG-TERM LOAN (use minus sign to make an extra loan payment; Enter $ no comma)** $_____

16. **DIVIDENDS DECLARED (total dollars to be paid; lack of profits will void)** $_____

17. **NINETY-TWO DAY CERTIFICATE OF DEPOSIT PURCHASED** (Enter in $ no comma)$_____

VERIFICATION TOTAL FOR ITEMS 1 to 17   [_____]

Notes: 1. Verification Total is for computer entry verification only. Include items 1 to 17. Subtract negative numbers. (2) All items except #5 to be entered each quarter even if there is no change. (3) Loan payment in addition to automatic payment.

Co #___ Ind___ Qtr#___   **AIRLINE DECISION FORM**

FIRST ACQUISITION TRANSACTION:
18. Number of Aircraft (0 - 4)   _____   (See page 12)
19. Type of Aircraft (A - G)   _____
20. Lease (1) or Purchase (2)   _____

SECOND ACQUISITION TRANSACTION:
21. Number of Aircraft (0 - 4)   _____
22. Type of Aircraft (A - G)   _____
23. Lease (1) or Purchase (2)_   _____

24. Serial Number of First Aircraft Disposal   _____   (Use this space first if disposing. See page 14)
25. Serial Number of Second Aircraft Disposal   _____
26. Serial Number of Third Aircraft Disposal   _____

27. Total Cost of Market Research Studies $_____   ($0 to 31000. See pg 14)

28. Incident Response   _____   (You <u>must</u> know the incident being used)

VERIFICATION TOTAL FOR ITEMS 18 to 28   [   ]
   NOTE: Verification Total is for computer entry
   verification only. Add all numbers.

29. CHANGES IN MARKETS SERVED: <u>Enter only the markets in which you have a change</u>. If changing any items in a currently held market, enter all items even though you may be changing only one item this period. Enter zeros beside a market you wish to abandon. A Fare Sale must be entered <u>each quarter</u> for each market if you wish to continue it.

	Market	Round Trip Flights per day	Total Seats (Flights times Seats on all A/C in this market)	Type of Fare Sale (0 - 3)
An Example >>	8	3	3-19 seat A/C=57	1
	_____	_____	_____	_____
	_____	_____	_____	_____
	_____	_____	_____	_____
	_____	_____	_____	_____
	_____	_____	_____	_____
	_____	_____	_____	_____
	_____	_____	_____	_____
	_____	_____	_____	_____
	_____	_____	_____	_____
	_____	_____	_____	_____
	_____	_____	_____	_____
	_____	_____	_____	_____
	_____	_____	_____	_____
	_____	_____	_____	_____

✔ **The most common error in completing the MARKETS SERVED form is to enter the number of seats on ONE aircraft and not multiply that number time the number of flights.**

MAXIMUM NUMBER OF MARKET CHANGES = 14. See page 14 for additional information.
© 2002 Software license requires new student manuals each semester used. Illegal to use otherwise.

Co #___ Ind___ Qtr#___ **AIRLINE DECISION FORM** Co Name_____

1. FARE (per seat mile flown) Groups: 28-31, 35-40, 48-51   Enter in cents (no decimal) _____

2. CABIN SERVICE   (Enter 0, 1, 2, or 3) _____
   Key: 0 = No in-flight service
       1 = Free Soft Drinks and Snacks
       2 = Free soft drinks, snacks, and a sandwich during mealtimes
       3 = Free drinks, hors d'oeuvres, meals

3. PROMOTION BUDGET   (Enter in $ with no comma) $_____

4. ADVERTISING BUDGET   (Enter in $ with no comma) $_____

5. NUMBER OF NEW SALESPERSONS HIRED <u>THIS QUARTER</u> (max 4 per quarter)   _____

6. EMPLOYEE COMPENSATION POLICY   Entry Key: _____
   Key: 0 = Pay minimum allowable by law or minimum prevailing wage
       1 = Managers and pilots receive ____% above minimum prevailing wage
       2 = Pay ____% above prevailing wage to pilots and professionals only.
       3 = Pay ____% above prevailing wage to all employees, including pilots and professionals
       4 = Pay ____% above prevailing wage to pilots and professionals + stock-bonus
       5 = Pay ____% above prevailing wage to all employees + stock-bonus (includes pilots and professionals)
       6 = Pay ____% above prevailing wage to pilots and professionals + 20% of profits
       7 = Pay ____% above minimum + 20% profits to all employees

7. Enter % wage increase (if applicable)   (no decimal) _____%

8. QUALITY PROGRAMS AND TRAINING (Enter in $ with no comma) $_____

9. MAINTENANCE LEVEL   (Enter Level 1, 2, or 3): _____
       Level 1: Legal minimum maintenance
       Level 2: Legal maintenance; additional 20% spare parts; wash every 3 months
       Level 3: Legal maintenance; additional 40% parts; Preventive Maintenance program; wash every month

10. FUEL CONTRACT for next quarter   Entry Key: _____
   Key: 0 = All fuel purchased on the spot market
       1 = 50% purchased on open market and 50% on contract
       2 = All fuel purchased on contract

11. CARGO MARKETING BUDGET (Minimum $10,000)   (Enter in $ no comma) $_____

12. CORPORATE SOCIAL PERFORMANCE BUDGET   (Enter in $ no comma) $_____

13. STOCK SOLD: In dollars, <u>not shares</u>   (Enter in $ no comma) $_____

14. SHORT-TERM LOAN (use a minus sign to make a loan payment; Enter in $ no comma) $_____

15. LONG-TERM LOAN (use minus sign to make an <u>extra</u> loan payment; Enter $ no comma) $_____

16. DIVIDENDS DECLARED (total dollars to be paid; lack of profits will void) $_____

17. NINETY-TWO DAY CERTIFICATE OF DEPOSIT PURCHASED   (Enter in $ no comma)$_____

VERIFICATION TOTAL FOR ITEMS 1 to 17   [   ]

Notes: 1. Verification Total is for computer entry verification only. Include items 1 to 17. Subtract negative numbers. (2) All items except #5 to be entered each quarter even if there is no change. (3) Loan payment in addition to automatic payment.

Co #___ Ind___ Qtr#___ **AIRLINE DECISION FORM**

FIRST ACQUISITION TRANSACTION:
18. Number of Aircraft (0 - 4)   _____ (See page 12)
19. Type of Aircraft (A - G)   _____
20. Lease (1) or Purchase (2)   _____

SECOND ACQUISITION TRANSACTION:
21. Number of Aircraft (0 - 4)   _____
22. Type of Aircraft (A - G)   _____
23. Lease (1) or Purchase (2)_   _____

24. Serial Number of First Aircraft Disposal   _____ (Use this space first if disposing. See page 14)
25. Serial Number of Second Aircraft Disposal   _____
26. Serial Number of Third Aircraft Disposal   _____

27. Total Cost of Market Research Studies $_____ ($0 to 31000. See pg 14)

28. Incident Response   _____ (You **must** know the incident being used)

VERIFICATION TOTAL FOR ITEMS 18 to 28   [   ]
     NOTE: Verification Total is for computer entry
            verification only. Add all numbers.

29. CHANGES IN MARKETS SERVED: Enter only the markets in which you have a change. If changing any items in a currently held market, enter all items even though you may be changing only one item this period. Enter zeros beside a market you wish to abandon. A Fare Sale must be entered each quarter for each market if you wish to continue it.

Market	Round Trip Flights per day	Total Seats (Flights times Seats on all A/C in this market)	Type of Fare Sale (0 - 3)
An Example >> 8	3	3-19 seat A/C=57	1
_____	_____	_____	_____
_____	_____	_____	_____
_____	_____	_____	_____
_____	_____	_____	_____
_____	_____	_____	_____
_____	_____	_____	_____
_____	_____	_____	_____
_____	_____	_____	_____
_____	_____	_____	_____
_____	_____	_____	_____
_____	_____	_____	_____
_____	_____	_____	_____

✔ **The most common error in completing the MARKETS SERVED form is to enter the number of seats on ONE aircraft and not multiply that number time the number of flights.**

MAXIMUM NUMBER OF MARKET CHANGES = 14. See page 14 for additional information.